QUESTION 7

Also by Richard Flanagan

The Living Sea of Waking Dreams
First Person
The Narrow Road to the Deep North
Wanting
The Unknown Terrorist
Gould's Book of Fish
The Sound of One Hand Clapping
Death of a River Guide

QUESTION 7

RICHARD FLANAGAN

Alfred A. Knopf
New York, 2024

THIS IS A BORZOI BOOK
PUBLISHED BY ALFRED A. KNOPF

www.aaknopf.com

Knopf, Borzoi Books, and the colophon are registered trademarks of Penguin Random House LLC.

Library of Congress Cataloging-in-Publication Data
Names: Flanagan, Richard, 1961– author.
Title: Question 7 / Richard Flanagan.
Other titles: Question seven
Description: First United States Edition. |
New York : Alfred A. Knopf, 2024.
Identifiers: LCCN 2023042980 (print) | LCCN 2023042981 (ebook) |
ISBN 9780593802335 (hardcover) | ISBN 9780593802342 (ebook)
Subjects: LCSH: Flanagan, Richard, 1961– | Flanagan, Richard, 1961– —Family. | Authors, Australian—Biography. | Families—Australia—Biography. | World War, 1939–1945—Prisoners and prisons, Japanese. | Prisoners of war—Japan—Biography. |
LCGFT: Autobiographies.
Classification: LCC PR9619.3.F525 Z46 2024 (print) |
LCC PR9619.3.F525 (ebook) | DDC 823 [B]—dc23/eng/20231005
LC record available at https://lccn.loc.gov/2023042980
LC ebook record available at https://lccn.loc.gov/2023042981

Jacket design by Adam Laszczuk, based on a painting by Dan Levenson

Manufactured in the United States of America
First American Edition

For Phil Cullen

The author has not given his effort here the benefit
of knowing whether it is history, autobiography,
gazetteer, tragedy, romance, almanac, melodrama,
or fantasy. It may be myriad, it may not.
The question is put, but where is the answer?

—HOBART TOWN MERCURY, reviewing MOBY-DICK, 1851

No, this is not piano. This is dreaming.

—DUKE ELLINGTON

One

1

In the winter of 2012, against my better judgement and for reasons that were not entirely to do with writing—much as I said they were—and which even now are not clear to me, I visited the site of Ohama Camp, Japan, where my father had once been interned. It was very cold, a bitter day, and an iron sky threw a foreboding cast on the Inland Sea beneath which my father had once worked in a coal mine as a slave labourer.

Nothing remained.

Though I had no wish to be bothered with it, I was taken to a local museum where a very helpful woman found numerous photographs documenting a detailed history of the coal mine from the early twentieth century—its growth, its processes, its Japanese workers.

There was no photograph of slave labourers.

The woman was kind and, as they say, *a fount of knowledge* about local history. She had never heard of slave labourers working at the Ohama coal mine. It was as if it had never happened, as if no one had ever been beaten or killed or made to stand naked in the snow until they died. I remember the woman's tolerant smile: a smile of pity for me thinking there had ever been slave labourers at the Ohama coal mine.

2

Sometimes I wonder why we keep returning to beginnings—why we seek the single thread we might pull to unravel the tapestry we call our life in the hope that behind it we will find the truth of *why*.

But there is no truth. There is only *why*. And when we look closer we see that behind that *why* is just another tapestry.

And behind it another, and another, until we arrive at oblivion.

3

At 8:15 a.m. on 6 August 1945, bombardier Major Thomas Ferebee released a lever 31,000 feet over Hiroshima, said "Bomb away!," and forty-three seconds later 60,000 people died while eighty miles to the south my father, a near-naked slave labourer in his fourth year of captivity as a prisoner of war, continued with his gruelling work pushing carriages of rock up long dark tunnels that ran under the Inland Sea.

Broken, ill, body and will near the end, knowing only that when in a few months the winter cold returned he could no longer endure and would die, he was unaware that he was now going to live. As my father made his way along the bleak mine tunnel only very occasionally punctuated with dim electric light bulbs a fellow Tasmanian POW remarked that it looked like his hometown of Penguin on a Friday night.

4

At the mine-head entrance, where my father and his fellow slave labourers once ran the gauntlet of guards who beat them as they passed, there now stood a love hotel. There was no memorial, no sign, no evidence, in other words, that whatever had once happened had ever happened. There was some neon signage. There was a business that catered for quick opportunistic sex in tiny rooms that allowed for sexual release and deliberately little else. What remained, or rather what existed, was only the oblivion of pleasure in another's arms—the same oblivion that simultaneously prefigures and denies death. As if the need to forget is as strong as the need to remember. Perhaps stronger.

And after oblivion? We return to the stories we

call our memories, perplexed, strangers to the ongoing invention that is our life.

5

Next to me that bitter day there stood an elderly Japanese man, Mr. Sato. He was tiny and frail, neatly dressed in a sports blazer and dress pants too long in the cuff from where, I assumed, he had shrunk with the passing of years. His hands were covered in thin white cotton gloves, and when he pointed out some long-vanished feature of the camp and mine below, all I saw was a loose thread dangling from the glove's cuff. I don't remember his shoes.

Mr. Sato's head came to my chest. He lived and cared for a daughter who, I was told by the translator, was very disabled. Mr. Sato had once been a guard at Ohama Camp. He showed me where the barracks had been, the farm up the hill, the mine head downhill, closer to the sea.

In front of us, to my embarrassment and unspoken anger, were a TV crew and several photographers from local newspapers. I had gone through a series of contacts to be at the mine head, and somehow the local council had become involved. Without my knowledge they had asked the media along. The TV crew and newspaper journalists wanted one thing: Mr. Sato and I embracing, an image of forgiveness, of understanding, of time healing. That would be, I knew, a lie. It wasn't for me to forgive.

Does time heal? Time does not always heal. Time scars. Mr. Sato's gloved hand was raised, pointing, the cold world below bisected by an unravelling thread.

6

Earlier that day I had met local, elderly villagers who had been children during the war. I had not wanted to meet them. I felt—how can I put this?—ashamed. My shame was perhaps that my return might be misunderstood as vengeance or anger. But I didn't know what my return was. They had been children and I had not then existed. I felt, in short, unequal to them and their lives. Maybe I was ashamed, somehow, of being my father's son presuming that his and their history might also be mine. I worried I might be seen as an unwelcome ghost, a spectre looking over the scene of an unsolved crime in which I was implicated. But the ghost of whom?—the murdered, the murderer or the witness, or all three?

Because it was an arrangement made by others I didn't know how to cancel it without causing offence. The elderly villagers were friendly, warm people. When telling their tales of the wartime privations they had endured as the children of the rural poor, they recalled the dissonance between what the adult world said and what as children they saw, and a childish irreverence took hold of those old voices and weathered faces. They remembered when the POWs had disembarked in late 1944, how the devils they had been taught to fear for so long were no more than pitiful, near-naked skeletons. As well as the cruelty of the Japanese guards, my father had spoken of the kindness of the Japanese miners, some of whom may have been these elderly villagers' fathers, who would share their meagre food with the starving POWs.

7

When I left school I worked as a chainman, the name given to a surveyor's labourer, a job centuries old set to vanish only a few years later with the advent of digital technology. It was the chainman's job to drag the twenty-two-yard chain with its hundred links with which the world was measured. By my time, the measuring chain was a thin steel band fifty metres long, but little else had changed from a century before. The chainman still carried a slash hook and axe to clear the survey lines of scrub and trees, and a whetstone and file to keep both sharp. I learnt to look out for evidence of old surveys from many decades before—collapsing stone cairns, rotting pegs, or the vulva form of bark on old eucalyptus trees. With the axe I would carefully scarf away the bark until what was revealed was a deep prism-shaped cavity skilfully hewed into the tree trunk long ago, sometimes over a century before. The apex of the inverted prism was the survey point.

I would stare at the marvel of that unaltered wound, the exact same as the day it was hewed by another axe. Time hadn't healed the tree, only scarred it, hiding something that was still happening. For beneath the scar the wound remained, a portal to the past bleeding fresh sap in the present, into which, if I stared for too long, I would feel myself falling.

Standing there that day in front of a Japanese TV crew with its young woman reporter, the handful of local photographers and bored journalists determined to get the only story that made sense and get out, was a similar moment of accelerating velocity. I had no desire to embrace Mr. Sato. Perhaps he felt the same. But not wishing to embarrass him or anyone else I put my arm around him and he around me. Everyone seemed happy with this.

When the photos and filming were done I let my arm drop. Mr. Sato remained curling into me. When I went to move away, his head seemed to slump into my chest. And so there we stood.

Perhaps he too was falling through some infinite void, or perhaps it was just the cold. I had no idea. I can't say I liked him holding me that way, this man who may once have beaten my father, but nor did I know how to be rid of him, to withdraw the warm comfort of my body.

I thought of Mr. Sato suffering with his disabled child and how at the end of his life he was being rightly punished. Then I felt ashamed thinking such a thing, aware that beneath this thought lay another I didn't wish to acknowledge. I looked away to the trees, bare, sad scrags; the earth unloved and cold around them, the rank grasses and weeds wretched-looking and lost. All of nature there seemed exhausted and disordered and me somehow a part of it. Below, the sea could be heard rolling in and out along its stony coast, as it always had and always would, concertinaing through the crimes and sins and loves and passions of those who passed through this sad country. My whole trip felt as incomprehensible as that sound of rocks rolling into oblivion.

Would I have done the same as Mr. Sato? And when I tried to push that question away another arose. If Mr. Sato, who seemed a decent man, was capable of being a guard, doing evil or just standing by when evil was done, would I be any different? Would I too join in beating the prisoners, even though I didn't wish to, would I too order a naked man to freeze to death kneeling in the falling snow, because it was what was expected, because it was too hard to say no? Or would I look away and choose not to help him? Then I lost the thread of my thoughts. The day was going. I thought of the prisoner made to kneel in the snow overnight without clothes, a story that had always left my father indescribably sad in its pointlessness. Would I do the same? I suddenly hated Mr. Sato's embrace and I hated Mr. Sato with all my being as he continued to lean on me. A cold wind blew and petered away. Afterwards it only felt that much colder, the sea continued rolling in and out, we no longer noticed each other, it occurred to me that neither of us had any idea what the other was thinking or feeling, how standing there we could have been mistaken as brothers or lovers.

We stood for a very long time as the journalists and TV crew departed, as dark clouds hastily gathered above us, seeming to shudder in unknown judgement and quickly disperse in their disappointment, as the Inland Sea reflected back to me only its own mystery. What had happened? To this day I have no idea. There is no why.

8

Is it because we see our world only darkly that we surround ourselves with lies we call time, history, reality, memory, detail, facts? What if time were plural and so were we? What if we discovered we begin tomorrow and we died yesterday, that we were born out of the deaths of others and life is breathed into us from stories we invent out of songs, collages of jokes and riddles and other fragments?

My father used to laugh about one of his fellow POWs who spoke of having seen the atomic bomb blast light up the night sky over their camp as if it were day.

The atomic bomb over Hiroshima exploded at 8:16 in the morning. The past is always most clearly seen by those who never saw it.

9

By the time Thomas Ferebee released the lever over Hiroshima, my father had somehow survived more than three years of Japanese internment. He had somehow survived Changi and the Death Railway. He had somehow survived the so-called Hell Ships that took the survivors of the Death Railway to Japan in the autumn of 1944, crammed into unseaworthy hulks without superstructures. Crowded within their rusting hulls, near-naked men endured typhoons, torpedoing by US submarines and strafing by US planes. By the time they landed on the island of Honshu the dream of a Japanese empire had turned into the imminent prospect of an invasion of Japan itself and what the Japanese military regime now called for in response: the mass suicide of 100 million Japanese, a nation reinvented as a death cult.

When the invasion happened, the Japanese civilian population was to defend the motherland with their lives. On Okinawa, the only Japanese island to be invaded, an estimated 150,000 civilians died. Mass suicides of civilians were common, some voluntary, many coerced at gunpoint by Japanese soldiers. In some instances, children killed their own parents when they showed insufficient enthusiasm at the prospect of death, and in other instances parents killed their own children.[1] When the lives of ordinary Japanese meant so little to their leaders it is no surprise that the lives of their enemy were meaningless: the Japanese were ready to massacre the 32,000 POW slave labourers in Japan when the invasion began.

The Americans planned to begin the final assault on Japan with the invasion of the island of Kyushu on 1 November 1945, to be followed by the invasion of Honshu in March 1946. Most likely my father would have been already dead by then, but if he had still been alive he would have been murdered. If, somehow, he had escaped that fate—though how that might have been possible it is hard to say—he did not believe he would have survived another bitter winter.

The Americans never invaded. Instead, they dropped the atom bomb. Sixty thousand people died in an instant, many more died slowly, agonisingly, over the succeeding hours and days, and they kept dying in the months and years that followed. Three days later the Americans dropped a second atomic bomb. Forty thousand people died in an instant, many more died slowly, agonisingly, over the succeeding hours and days, and they kept dying in the months and years that followed.

10

Fifteen years and eleven months later the fifth of my father's six children was born on a hard winter's morning. He was to be called Daniel, but the Irish Catholic nuns at Longford's Carmelite convent told my mother that Daniel was too Catholic and too Irish and too common a name. A shame job, as they say. But we were too Catholic and too Irish and too common for a shame job not to matter. And so I was named Richard. My father hated his name by which he later found himself loved and so too have I hated mine, but we, my name and I, have grown and entwined around each other until like old roots it's hard to say where one ends and the other begins. Every old sock, as my father would sometimes say about odd couples, finds an old boot.

11

That night it began to rain heavily, the sort of rain that seems weighted with coins when you are compelled to move through it, making any room you enter feel light. I was taken to a hostess bar in Sanyo-Onoda City by Kenji Y—, the Sanyo-Onoda Council's International Affairs and Equal Opportunities officer. Kenji Y— wore slightly ill-fitting office clothes that bespoke a man who went about the duties of his office with the good spirits and bemusement of one whose heart was elsewhere but happily so. He seemed content in the name of making a living to fill in the hours allotted as work, tending to whatever absurdity, such as myself, he encountered along the way. Kenji Y— loved his wife and child, and he liked mountain biking. Things that were not straightforward perplexed him, but he sensed truth even when he didn't fully apprehend it. There was about him a kindness.

Kenji Y— told me how his grandfather had fought in the war in the charnel house that was New Guinea. On his return he had great difficulty relating to his family. He had built a hut in the mountains where he lived alone for increasingly extended periods. He drank.

"Did they know why he was that way?" I asked.

"No," Kenji Y— said, "he never talked about it."

"Did he speak of the war?" I asked.

"No," Kenji Y— said, "he never spoke of the war."

"They say New Guinea was hell," I said.

"He never talked about it," Kenji Y— said.

The hostess bar was a warm room with a few office types—all salarymen—being served drinks by the hostesses, young, heavily made-up women with anime eyes, whose job it was to strike postures of amusement and interest in individual men who didn't seem all that interesting or amusing as they became excessively drunk on the local sweet potato vodka. The rain continued falling, but in a muted, distant way as when you are falling asleep and drifting into another world.

12

One hostess, a small woman, spoke English and so it fell to her to sit with me. She asked me what I was doing in Sanyo-Onoda City. She was nice or she was very good in a professional way at appearing to be nice. In any case, it seemed important to be nice in return though it was clear not many tourists came to Sanyo-Onoda City and it was hard to know what being nice meant in this context. I replied I was a writer doing research for a book. That was, as I think I have said already, both true and untrue. Increasingly I didn't understand why I was there at all because none of it would ever appear in the book I was writing. That I was a writer interested her, or seemed to interest her, as she said she liked books. What was my book about? she asked.

I wasn't sure what my book was about. I may have said something about love, which had the virtue of not being untrue and being so broad as to be meaningless. She raised a hand to her mouth and politely laughed behind it. I sensed that for her Sanyo-Onoda City and love were not ideas that naturally ran in tandem. She smiled again and repeated her original question: so why was I in Sanyo-Onoda City?

To our side a few steps away, Kenji Y—, now very drunk, was bellowing out a karaoke love ballad into a microphone. No one was listening. Perhaps that was the point of the hostess bar, I thought. You sang your heart out and no one noticed, you talked from the bottom of your heart and no one listened.

I looked back at her. I said that I was visiting the place where my father once worked as a slave labourer.

She looked up at me with her dreamy anime eyes and blinked. Still smiling, she said, "What is *slave labourer*?"

13

She kept smiling, fixed as if in a rictus. For that matter, the whole world felt fixed in a rictus, and me with it. As if we both were now in a kabuki performance I smiled back and kept smiling and she kept smiling and I kept smiling and it was hard to believe, or think, as I felt all the sadness in the world fill me at that moment: for Mr. Sato leaning into me, for my father, for the smiling Japanese hostess with anime eyes, for everyone in that overly warm bar and in the world that brutally cold, wet night.

I thought of Kenji Y—'s grandfather alone in his rude hut in the mountains unable to find words, as I was now unable to find words that might express any of it. Kenji's grandfather had been walking with ghosts. Perhaps, like me, he was already becoming one himself before he died, inhabiting a world that had no knowledge nor desire to know what had happened. Somewhere there was a real world where all that passed continued to exist. But it was not here, and strangely that seemed at once a relief and a horror. Nothing I said could be heard nor anything I saw seen, and together, Kenji Y—'s grandfather and me, we kept staring into time, knowing only what had happened was always happening and would never stop happening.

I looked into that young woman's eyes.

"Nothing important," I said.

There was a tap on my shoulder. It was Kenji Y—. Did I want to sing something?

14

It could be argued that science was inexorably heading towards the discovery of nuclear fission and therefore the invention of the atomic bomb and thus Hiroshima. But nothing is ever inevitable, least of all the atomic bomb in the mid-twentieth century, a project which, as one of its key theorists, Niels Bohr, the Danish physicist, noted, would only happen if someone could turn a country into a single workshop devoted to that task.

At a high-level Nazi conference on 4 June 1942 Niels Bohr's former student, the brilliant German physicist Werner Heisenberg, spoke of a bomb no bigger than a pineapple capable of destroying a city. But after, when Albert Speer questioned Heisenberg, he found the physicist's answers "by no means encouraging . . . The technical prerequisites for production would take years to develop, two years at the earliest, even provided the program was given maximum support."

Speer reported back to Hitler.

"Hitler had sometime spoken about the possibility of an atom bomb, but the idea quite obviously strained his intellectual capacity. He was also unable to grasp the revolutionary nature of nuclear physics. In the twenty-two-hundred recorded points of my conferences with Hitler," Speer continued in his exhaustive, exhausting manner, "nuclear fission comes up only once, and then is mentioned with extreme brevity. Hitler did sometimes comment on its prospects, but what I told him of conferences with the physicists confirmed his view that there was not much profit in the matter."

When Hitler heard that Heisenberg had not given any final answer to Speer's question as to whether nuclear fission could be kept under control he was "not delighted with the possibility that the earth under his rule might be transformed into a glowing star."

By the time Heisenberg was describing the possibility of pineapple-size atomic bombs, the war was turning against the Nazis in Russia, and any project needed to be able to promise certainty of benefit. Because Hitler remained convinced he would defeat both the Soviet Union and Britain by 1943, there was a standing rule that only weaponry that could be battle-ready within an eighteen-month window be supported. Presented with the possibility of an atom bomb, Germany turned away from it, believing it would take too long to develop, particularly when the result—an atom bomb that actually worked—was by no means guaranteed.

After the Nazis abandoned research on the bomb, they devoted limited resources to developing a "uranium motor," which would become known in the United States as a nuclear reactor. They failed in this also. At war's end the leading German nuclear scientists were nevertheless captured and put in an English manor house near Cambridge to discover what they did and didn't know. Treated as guests and shown every courtesy, they were unaware that all the bedrooms and living rooms had been bugged. Shortly before dinner on 6 August 1945 they were told that an atom bomb had been built and exploded by the Allies over Hiroshima.

15

At first the German scientists were disbelieving that the backward, vulgar Americans could accomplish what German civilisation could not. As more confirmations were made, though, their disdain transformed into anger then, finally, a virtuous horror—not without its own self-serving hypocrisy—that such a weapon would be created, the use of which as civilised men they found disgusting and abhorrent.

Their conversations continued: a confusion of professional affront soothed by moral grandstanding, attempts to tease out whether they were building the bomb for the sake of the motherland or for the sake of Nazism, or, for that matter, whether they had ever been serious about building a bomb at all.

The German scientists' doubts about the project, their own abilities, and their very intentions grew as their misgivings and sheer bewilderment multiplied. Could they have built the bomb? *Would* they have built the bomb? Had they ever even intended to build the bomb? Was their failure failure or was their failure a unique form of passive resistance? Was their failure *their* failure or was it their unspoken triumph—or was it, after all, the fault of their leaders?

> *Paul Harteck (physical chemist):* We might have succeeded if the highest authorities had said, "We are prepared to sacrifice everything."
>
> *Carl Friedrich von Weizsäcker (physicist):* In our case even the scientists said it couldn't be done.
>
> *Erich Bagge (physicist):* That's not true. You were there yourself at that conference in Berlin. I think it was on 8 September that everyone was asked—Geiger, Bothe, and you, Harteck, were there too, and everyone said that it must be done at once. Someone said, "Of course it is an open question whether one ought to do a thing like that." Thereupon Bothe got up and said, "Gentlemen, it must be done." Then Geiger got up and said, "If there is the slightest chance that it is possible—it must be done." That was on 8 September '39 . . .[2]

16

Perhaps the only country capable of inventing and producing a workable bomb in the mid-twentieth century was the only country that could manage such a massive diversion of its economy—the United States of America. Over the course of the war, under the auspices of the highly secret Manhattan Project, it turned much of its resources—the equivalent of what was flowing into the car industry at the time in terms of investment, the labour of more than half a million workers and the genius of thousands of scientists—into a single workshop with a single goal: the creation of the atom bomb.

"Bomb away!" said Thomas Ferebee at 8:15 a.m. on 6 August 1945, releasing a lever 31,000 feet over Hiroshima. The B-29's bomb bay doors fell open and an atom bomb codenamed Little Boy dropped out of its belly, triggering an intricate sequence of successive tripwires, electrical plugs, timers, barometric fuses and altimeters. Forty-three seconds later, at 1,900 feet above ground level, a final circuit closed and four silk powder bags each containing two pounds of cordite were detonated by a tiny explosion that in turn initiated the largest man-made explosion in human history. And then the four silk powder bags were no more than vapour and energy along with the 60,000 Japanese souls ascending with them to heaven.

That's life.

17

I say 60,000 souls because that was the initial figure put on the initial dead. But no one knows how many people died in that instant or subsequently. Everyone who has sought to quantify how many people died at Hiroshima has qualified their estimate by admitting it is impossible to know how many people died at Hiroshima. As well as 60,000 dead another official estimate says 80,000 dead and another official estimate says 140,000 dead and all three estimates are authoritative and all are heavily qualified and in truth no one actually knows. Nor does anyone agree on why the war ended. No one agrees on why the war started either. No one agrees, no one knows, and all that can be said with absolute certainty is that soaring as pure energy and vaporised fragments towards the heavens that morning amidst animals, buildings, road signs, carts, cars, trams, so many numberless human beings and so much assorted detritus of daily living were four silk powder bags.

What remains of Hiroshima that day are only questions.

Do possibly more corpses tomorrow justify possibly fewer corpses today? We pretend to have the answers to this sort of thing. We pretend we know. We pretend there is a moral calculus in war. We pretend so many things. In war, though, not even simple arithmetic is possible. In recent times we have become prisoners of the idea that life is infinitely measurable, that all human wanting and torment and laughter, all hate and all love, can be reduced to that contemporary word *metrics.* That there is, in other words, an answer for all things that can be found in numbers.

But the elusiveness of those innumerable unknown souls on that blue morning defies measurement and mocks metrics. They exist outside of numbers. Chekhov believed that the role of literature was not to provide answers but only to ask the necessary questions. One of Chekhov's earliest stories was a parody of mental arithmetic questions asked of schoolchildren, of which Chekhov's question 7 is typical:

> Wednesday, June 17, 1881, a train had to leave station A at 3 a.m. in order to reach station B at 11 p.m.; just as the train was about to depart, however, an order came that the train had to reach station B by 7 p.m. Who loves longer, a man or a woman?[3]

Who?

You, me, a Hiroshima resident or a slave labourer? And why do we do what we do to each other?

That's question 7.

18

Who loves longer?

Though written for money at the very start of his career, question 7 is in many ways the archetypal Chekhov story in just two sentences. Like so much of what Chekhov wrote, question 7 is about how the world from which we presume to derive meaning and purpose is not the true world. It is a surface world, a superficial world, a frozen world of appearances, beneath which an entirely different world surges as if a wild river that at any moment might drown us. A woman ignored at dinner tables, a chorus girl betrayed, a man who deludes himself he is happier in the country, a womaniser who pretends to himself that he is not falling in love, a grieving cab man who tries to tell each of his fares his son has just died only to be ignored, and who ends up finding the only one who has time to listen is his horse; so much falsity beneath which we discover only in the last paragraphs, or sometimes even the last sentence, the truth of these people and through them of life itself.

Virtue and morality are stripped away to reveal cruelty and wickedness while cruelty and wickedness, in turn, are stripped away to reveal kindness and goodness. As in life, we are shocked. There is something sacrilegious about Chekhov, something shocking in his gentle, unassuming stories, so seemingly plain, that finally refuse to accept the logic of this world and always surprise us by revealing another world that we recognise as the real world in which we live.

Who loves longer? Chekhov's genius lay in never presuming to give the answer. Of Tolstoy's *Anna Karenina* Chekhov merely said it framed the questions correctly. Each of us has a public life and private life. But beyond both is a secret life that baffles us. Perhaps the only reply that can be made to Hiroshima is to ask question 7. If it is a question that can never be answered, it is still the question we must keep asking, if only in order to understand that life is never binary, nor reducible to cant or code, but a mystery we at best apprehend. In Chekhov's stories, the only fools are those with answers.

19

The United States only did what it did creating the atom bomb because a man called Leo Szilard, haunted by questions, persuaded its president it should and then helped make the impossible possible. And Leo Szilard only did what he did because he had once read a novel. The novel was written out of a terror of love and it terrified Leo Szilard and entranced him in equal measure until it became his destiny. The novel was written by H. G. Wells.

20

H. G. Wells looked up from the book he was reading at the woman who had just entered the room. She was even younger than he had been led to believe. The book was a discourse on the latest discoveries about radium by Frederick Soddy. The ideas in it physically excited Wells in a manner akin to sex which he also found exciting and, when he thought about it, it had to be said more so. Except he did not think so when he thought about it objectively, that is to say scientifically, that is to say rationally, for at such times he found his thoughts, normally so clear, so assured and confident, would grow oddly muddy, equally bewildered and bewildering on such matters, as the knots of feeling, rather than unravelling through reason, only pulled tighter.

In his life he slept with whom he wished, feeling not that he was unfaithful to his wife but rather, as he explained to her, that he was faithful to his philosophy. After all, it was 1912. In his thoughts Wells sought to square sexual freedom with rationality and social utility. He was developing a theory of the "lover-shadow" to explain his actions as a necessary social good and perhaps the very basis of society, but it never seemed to quite get beyond some muddled conceptions. In his dreams he walked on ice in glass-soled shoes with predictable results.

Still, he felt, with some pride, that he had never allowed sex to dominate his scientific curiosities, his politico-social urges, or his sense of obligation. Yet nor would he suppress sex, suppression being anathema to him. He did what he pleased, freed, he felt, by vocation, from the prohibitions that fell on the lawyer, doctor and schoolteacher. He supposed most other men had as much or more drive, but less outlet. He had begun to ask himself, "Why not?" Hearing no answer in the negative, he did as he pleased. He couldn't ever quite explain it satisfactorily but then who ever had? He liked to fuck and he could and so he did. Perhaps there was more to it; he spent hours failing to work out what that might be, while the truth was women made him quiver like a fish and the one now smiling at him from the sitting room door—top teeth slightly prominent in her gypsy face and her bottom somewhat more prominent in a blue silk hobble skirt—electrified him. She was a question mark he intended to answer.

21

The young woman standing before him was Cicely Fairfield, a failed actress who had only recently taken up journalism. She struck a dishevelled and disreputable pose. She found it to her advantage but within a few years she would drop it, coming to believe that in old age it was seen to prefigure only death. And the young woman intended to live: long, largely, making her mark in her own way.

Cicely Fairfield was revelling in a moment of metamorphosis. She affected a world weariness far beyond her years. To help the effect along she had stolen for her nom de plume the name of a character from a fashionable Ibsen play—a prototype New Woman, an alpha female adventuress, with a Christian name as old as the Bible and a surname as unwavering as a lodestone. Within a year of adopting it she had found a distinctive voice as a writer, a sting and charm enlivened by the gift for sometimes surreal metaphors, a talent that decades later would see her celebrated as the most important "woman writer" in the English language.

She discovered very early that her chief strength as a writer was that she wrote as she felt, whereas most writers only write as others think. Along with her new name she stole from Ibsen the thoroughly non-English idea that ideas make the world spin around, and saved herself from the hubris of this fancy by having no original ideas of her own but only a gift for a certain ferocity of observation about those who did.

Fittingly, she began her new career with book reviews, a perfect place to leapfrog to an elevated position on the shoulders of the famous she sat on and shat on. Her reviews were enlivened by a passing acquaintanceship with the writings of a newly fashionable philosopher called Friedrich Nietzsche, thrilling more to the vigour of the German's prose than engaging with his thought. Befitting her new androgynous persona as a feminist *Ubermensch,* she took from Nietzsche a literary absolutism she made her personal style. If her literary judgements were not always of the first order, choosing to praise the inconsequential and now forgotten, the fierce sting and wild daring were most on display, most telling and most winning, when she went hunting for the biggest names to bring down. Her scandalous attacks delighted readers and were making her famous.

The young woman sensed she had arrived at one of those cusps of time where history creaks and cracks like a glacier calving an iceberg. She was the voice of the New defining itself by revealing the Old as ripe for mockery and derision. If not an original game she gave it a new edge by virtue of her sex and the dexterity of her attacks, as pointed as a poisoned dart. The times were hers, and when she turned her gaze on the time traveller, future's prophet himself, Mr. H. G. Wells, she humiliated him for having been only ever about the past.

Rebecca West was nineteen.

22

For his part Bertie Wells had long ago ceased being Bertie and was now not even a name but merely two initials, the same initials that adorned his book jackets and spines and introduced his surname: H. G.—the very same H. G. Wells, one of the most famous writers in the Empire, of whose latest novel only a week before Rebecca West had written a scathing review in the radical feminist magazine *The Freewoman,* to which Wells was also an occasional contributor.

"Mr. Wells's mannerisms are more infuriating than ever in *Marriage,*" the review began, words that Rebecca West was to discover could serve as a personal as well as a literary judgement.

For Wells was at once as notoriously devoted to his domestic life with his second wife, Jane, as he was to his affairs—most scandalously with twenty-one-year-old Amber Reeves, daughter of prominent Fabians, with whom he had a daughter; most recently with Elizabeth von Arnim, the celebrated Australian-born author and wife of a German aristocrat who had become famous for her books about her travails on her Pomeranian estate and her seeking to become part of the Junker aristocracy. The people's prophet of change was in his private life master of only a curious stasis.

H. G. Wells was forty-six.

23

If not a vertiginous low, Wells's career had hit a complacent lull. After the late Victorian sensations of *The Time Machine, The War of the Worlds* and *The Island of Dr. Moreau,* he had turned away from his scientific romances, as they were called, to more conventional storytelling and written a series of books that had not always been so well received. For every *Tono-Bungay* and *The History of Mr. Polly*—both popular successes, if not of the same order as the earlier books—there was an *Ann Veronica*, deemed so scandalous that Wells had to find a new publisher after his own turned it down, and *The New Machiavelli.* Both acquired their notoriety as fictionalised versions of Wells's affair with Amber Reeves.

In both books Wells had coupled a denunciation of Victorian morality to a spirited defence of sexual freedom. And yet because he kept up a conventional bourgeois life with his wife and two sons he was at once identified enough with the old order to be worth Rebecca West taking down, and sufficiently of the new to offer salacious material to help her do so.

"Of course," she continued needling, "he is the old maid among novelists; even his sex-obsession that lay clotted over *Ann Veronica* and *The New Machiavelli* like cold white sauce was merely an old maid's mania, the reaction towards the flesh of a mind too long absorbed in airships."

And there it was for the world to see—all pure energy she; all putrid entropy he. Cold white sauce indeed. In his most vivid passages Wells had imagined a future world in which a dimming, exhausted sun feebly illuminated a few remnant monsters as energy came to its end: it was his recurrent nightmare and not only of the world. A dimming star himself, how could he not be intrigued by the possibility of a new energy source, be it Soddy's radium or the young woman in the fetching skirt?

Wells didn't know whether he was offended or intrigued or both when he read her savaging of his work. But he had read enough and heard enough to want to meet her. And so he invited Rebecca West to lunch.

24

On the day, Rebecca West chose to wear a blue silk hobble skirt she had borrowed from a friend several months before and was yet to return. Perhaps, she thought, she never would return the skirt. She liked it, she liked the way it clutched her thighs, liked how it made her feel and the attention it drew, and she liked how it simultaneously attracted and confused men who expected her to turn up in pantaloons or some such suffragette nonsense. She thought of it as her Rebecca West skirt. Only now, as she stepped out of the hansom cab she couldn't afford but had felt obliged to arrive in, did she see that the hem was slightly frayed. Perhaps she would return it.

She reached inside her handbag and, not without difficulty given the skirt's constricting cut, squatted down and snipped the offending threads back to a temporary straight line with a pair of nail scissors. Focusing on the cutting, she noticed her fingernails were dirty. She ran them under her teeth, spat on the pavement, and opened the gate to H. G. Wells's home.

The housekeeper who ushered the exotic, wild, shabby and sharp young woman inside to meet the Wellses later told the butler that she felt like she was serving a lamb roast to a wolf, except for once it wasn't entirely clear who was the lamb.

Rebecca West followed the housekeeper to a sitting room where she was met by an attractive middle-aged woman who turned out to be Wells's wife, who introduced herself in the informal modern fashion as Jane. It was irritating. In the library to which she was next led was Wells himself, and as he rose from his chair to meet her, it was, Rebecca West had to admit, a shock. For having eviscerated Wells's writings with words, Rebecca West was unprepared in every way for what she met in the flesh that day.

The man described as *a giant* turned out to be very short. For someone about whom words such as *the future* and *energy* were routinely used he appeared to be ageing badly, and dumpy with it. He exuded an earthy odour when he spoke. His eyes, so often pronounced as belonging to a visionary, seemed to her colourless, watery things housed beneath hapless drooping eyelids that suggested some rare breed of poultry. He was, quite simply, one of the ugliest men she had ever met.

25

Thankfully he began talking. He was a torrent of words—the woman question? Suffrage? Anarcho-syndicalism in the Rhondda? Her exact thoughts on Mrs. Humphry Ward? The Pankhursts? Dora Marsden? The rapidly changing nature of women's fashions and the gender confusions of some new styles on both men's and women's parts—and all larded with low gossip, high science and startling opinions.

Charming as Jane Wells was, she soon withdrew—she seemed a little effaced, Rebecca West felt, sensing a small victory—leaving the two writers alone to talk. And for the best part of the next five hours, they did just that. If there was something abject about him physically, something absurd about a voice so comically thin and high-pitched it put her in mind of a drowning tin whistle, Wells still seemed to take her seriously, more seriously than any man ever had. Listening to his relentless flow of incoming ideas, questions to which she had no immediate answers, she felt like a telephone switchboard operator taking a barrage of calls without switching plugs. Still, that did not concern her. For if H.G. liked to explain, Rebecca liked to argue. She found herself beginning to warm to him. He was fascinating—and equally, she sensed, he was growing fascinated. It was not exactly conversation but something she felt was better. Women may be idiots, she thought, but men are lunatics. Intersecting monologues, that was the art and pleasure of being with him.

And so as their monologues began duelling, dancing, fighting and playing together, tumbling like dangerous kittens, she began enjoying herself. He would later call her Jaguar and she would call him Panther. While she could see he pretended to be a feminist but wasn't, she was still beguiled by his intellect, his world, his glittering life. She was falling and he with her, tumbling and falling, and a waltz as if played on a watery tin whistle was playing in her head faster and faster as everything began to swirl around them.

Within half an hour she knew there wasn't a man in all of England, in Europe even! who could compare. Not even the Belvedere Apollo could hold a candle to H.G., she thought, and she laughed at him and that funny little mouth with its crooked teeth grinned back.

For his part, Wells had never met anyone like Rebecca West and he very much doubted if there ever was anything like Rebecca West before. Many years later he would recall that she was mixed race, her mother hailing from the West Indies. This would seem without foundation but evoked the exoticism he found so attractive in her. She struck him as at once chappish and womanly. She talked like no one else, slowly weaving slightly grubby fingernails around her tales and ragged skirt as if she were an Andalusian dancer. She did these and other things in a fashion that Wells found vivacious and exciting all at once, using words as if they were fruit she had just picked straight from the tree, taken one bite from and then tossed over her shoulder.

She floated from the slave morality of Christianity to her family who, she said, were *vampiring* her; her father was glorious, she said, she had no father at all, she laughed; Mark Twain she adored and of Tolstoy she could not speak but only yawn except for the anti-sex thing which wasn't enough to justify risking asphyxiation reading *Anna Karenina*. The suffragettes she admired enormously, but their business about venereal diseases which were supposed to be around every corner, all up, seemed to her, though she wasn't in a position to judge, just a little silly.

The more he returned serve the more she came back with another ace. Wicked and wickedly clever, she had the qualities he lacked and feared the most and desired above everything else. He, the apostle of a free life, had been accused by Amber Reeves of somehow never living. But here, in this vivacious, wild-haired woman, was the very stuff of life.

A few weeks later they met again. Did the youthful Rebecca, not far distant from her acting days, searching towards her new role, now reenact the part of the heroine of Wells's *Ann Veronica,* the novel she had so recently rubbished? Did she tell Wells in Wells's own words, as he had Ann Veronica tell an older married man, that she wanted him to be her lover? Or was it Wells who pleaded with her?

All that is known is this: in front of his bookcase, while talking about matters of literary style, they kissed.

26

That kiss would, in time, beget death which would, in turn, beget me and the circumstances of my life that lead to the book you now hold, a chain reaction which began over a century ago, and all of which will lead to the unlikely figure of my father, unlikely in that he is to appear in a story with, among others unknown to him, H. G. Wells and Rebecca West.

In front of the bookcase they now pause and stare for a moment at each other, they smell each other, he of walnuts, she of lavender, both scents that she would come to associate with an inexorable longing and an incommunicable anger.

Their later accounts of this seminal event confused much but were certain on one thing: it was mutual. They both took what they wanted. Perhaps it was her. Perhaps it was him. Perhaps it is what remains when memory and obliteration collide: imagination. Perhaps it just was: inexplicable to both. Perhaps it was question 7.

Two

1

It was clear to me even when I was very young that my father was different, that he had passed through something, but what that something was wasn't ever really talked about. A quiet and reserved man who neither disciplined me nor encouraged me nor damned me nor praised me, he was for the most part vaporous, there and not there, substance and non-substance.

He saw the world aslant. It was for him a great tragicomedy in which the comedy was made poignant by the tragedy and the tragedy rendered bearable by the comedy. When the subject was sad or serious, he would smile wanly, his face turning inside out, a concertina of wrinkles compressing his eyes into wry sunken currants, and from him would flow a riversong of stories.

Even when I was young he already seemed impossibly old, so much older than other kids' fathers, and his mouth would form that slight smile and he would tell an anecdote about someone or other in Cleveland, the tiny Georgian coaching hamlet set in some raggedy woodland in the Tasmanian Midlands, where he had been born the month Germany invaded Belgium in 1914, and you would see the event, the tragedy, in some larger human light.

There was Doughy Bonner who boasted he could outrun the train, stripped off and running through the bush in his long underwear alongside the express to Hobart, only to lose, his figure forever flickering through the framing of skinny-trunked willow leaf eucalypts like a Mack Sennett silent comedy of the era. Mrs. Barker, so poor, who had never seen ice cream and with the last of her pennies bought seven ice-cream cones while visiting Launceston, one for each of her children, put them in her handbag and did it up, before catching the train back to Cleveland.

But of Rightio Burton who fell in the shit trough in Hintok and, too weak to escape, drowned, and of his dear mate Micky Hallam, dragged out of the camp hospital and beaten to death for no particular reason by the Japanese as the rest of the POWs were made to stand and watch, he could find few words nor even his customary wan smile. That's life.

2

One of the first things my father did when he made it home after the war ended was to take a train trip around all of Tasmania that he could visit. Perhaps he wanted to see people and places he had thought he would never see again. Perhaps it was an immeasurable comfort to him to be allowed to sit in their homes, their kitchens, their lounges, their backyards and say little or nothing, warmed by the human goodness of others, to be astonished by the small everyday acts of kindness too easily dismissed as everyday. He went to the rainforest, he went to the beaches. He went alone, touching his earth once more as if it were some sacrament necessary to live. None of these places had any value to the larger world, deemed without worth to commerce or justification by European art. But in the scrag ends of an island at the end of the world, in its unhonoured and unknown wonder, broken men rediscovered how to live.

To live, Gordon A—, neither a friend of my father nor a man for sentiment but another ex-POW, once told me how on returning he went up the remote Gordon and Franklin rivers and stayed put there amidst rainforest trees older than the great religions, working as a Huon pine sawyer, because, he said, he was sick and the rainforest rivers of the southwest were healing country.

To live, Clyde Mc—, an ex-POW mate, took a job skippering the *May Queen,* an old ketch that dated back to convict times, sailing it into the immense skies and aching serenity of Storm Bay, past the giant waves of Shipstern Bluff and the soaring cliffs of Cape Raoul, bringing and taking goods and supplies from the little towns that had grown out of the abandoned penal settlements along the way at Premaydena, Taranna, Nubeena and Carnarvon, listening to the scud and thump of the wooden bow rising and dropping through the indifferent ocean, the sound of dolphin trains broaching and rippling; laughing at the leaping jackknives of blue-fin tuna dappling the sky here! there! everywhere! as if crazily bouncing off some subterranean trampoline.

To live, Boy M— returned to trapping in the snow country where he was consoled by the cry of the currawong echoing through the ruby gold heathlands and snow drifts, eerie, ancient, defiant, the jo witties calling him home, h-o-o-o-o—*ome*! In their different ways, they all returned to the land and sea of their island home. To the healing country. To be healed.

To live.

3

There is a photo of my father taken before the war, aged twenty-four, with his father, mother and brother Tom. They look, as they were, irredeemably poor, his mother already wasted from the consumption that will shortly carry her away. He, however, taller, moody, handsome, looks dapper in a pair of Oxford bags and jacket. He doesn't belong and he seems to know it.

In his nineties, hospitalised after a heart attack, he told me how back then he had been ashamed of his family and their poverty. And now he, in turn, was ashamed of having had such thoughts. He loved them. His tragedy, he told me another time, was to leave the working class but never arrive in the middle class. His triumph, I see now, was to survive.

Shame lay like crusted blood over the island: when he returned from playing football in Hobart, the island's capital, to Launceston, its second and far richer city, through which the sheep money flowed and which identified much more with Victoria than Tasmania, he went into a drapery and asked for a shirt with a certain sort of lapel that he had seen in a Hobart shop window only to be told there was no such shirt. When my father insisted there was because he had seen it himself in Hobart, the shop assistant leant over the counter, repeated his claim that no such shirt ever existed, adding, "Listen, sonny, we're not a convict town like Hobart, we are part of Victoria, and I'm telling you—that shirt doesn't exist."

Experience is but a moment. Making sense of that moment is a life.

4

He was a sick man and an enigmatic man all through my childhood. An alone man. He suffered a range of non-specific health problems which were known in the family as Dad's ulcer. Dad's ulcer meant that unlike so many of his army mates he drank almost nothing in the way of alcohol, taking a bottle of milk rather than beer with him when he went to visit. He drank milk of magnesia for his ulcer, a compound that left glasses streaked with a chalky residue, which as a child I feared, as if it might carry the strange illness that left my father so thin and distant.

There is a photo of him that was taken when he finally left Longford, the town where I was born and where he was much loved. It ran on the front of the local paper. He stands, a tall, striking man neither young nor old, neither alone nor befriended, while a host of schoolchildren sit around him. It is a strange photo. He looks like a celebrity or movie star rather than a country schoolteacher. He rises out of the children like an edifice, not human and human at the same time. Warm and distant. Loved and alone. He smiles characteristically. Which is to say quizzically.

He once told me he'd had a dream in which he had died, and he is in his coffin being wheeled through Longford's streets and the whole town is out watching him as the coffin passes. And it was then, he said, that he knew he had to leave. He was admired. He lived, I sometimes think, looking at that photo, in an autumnal solitude. At the heart of his gentleness was the feeling that without kindness we are nothing. Kindness and courage: with him the two seemed synonyms. Perhaps it had been that way about him all his life.

5

One of the few times I saw him get angry as a child was when the American movie *King Rat* was to be shown on TV over the summer holidays and we wanted to watch it. My father refused to let us. I saw it later at a friend's home. Based on a highly successful American novel, *King Rat* tells of how an American POW prospers in the Changi POW camp by stealing from other POWs and running rackets and, as a successful criminal, becomes the de facto head of the camp.

My father said the camps weren't like that at all, that it was an American idea, and anyone who'd behaved like the King Rat character wouldn't have lasted. What he meant by not lasting he didn't say. It was the first time I ever really knew anything about the camps and my father. When I asked if he had been at Changi, he said not really, which was true as he had only passed through it en route to the Death Railway. No one had heard of the Death Railway in those days. Even then my father's world was not the real world which, it was evident from all the advertising around the Hollywood film, was that of a Hollywood film. My father despised *King Rat*. It was an American story. His was not.

His story was otherwise: we were told that on the Death Railway there was a POW camp of English not far from the Australians' camp at Hintok where my father was, and there the English divided on class lines, the officers not working, keeping the small stipend the Japanese inexplicably paid imprisoned officers for themselves and surviving, the enlisted men labouring and starving and in consequence *dying like flies*. His words. The Australians, he told us, held together as one, the officers being compelled to pool their stipend to buy drugs and food for the sick on the black market, and working in the camp hospital and kitchen to help the group. Together they survived—or at least far more of them than the English.

That was his story and that much we knew growing up. You went under alone but together you could survive. When someone was down you helped, not out of altruism, but an enlightened selfishness: this way we all have a chance. The measure of the strongest was also the only guarantee of ongoing strength: their capacity to help the weakest. Mateship wasn't a code of friendship. It was a code of survivors. It demanded you help those who are not your friends but who are your mates. It demanded you sacrifice for the group. Is that a convict idea? Is it an Indigenous idea? Is it both things merged? It's not a European or an American idea. It is, though, a deeply old, serious idea of humanity.

A book on the Death Railway, an oral history, names my father. A survivor recalled how at the height of the dreaded Speedo—when the monsoon and cholera reigned, exhaustion was a prelude to death, and the Japanese demanded the starving POWs work up to sixteen hours a day, seven days a week—Japanese trucks would sometimes of a night become bogged on the treacherous jungle tracks. The prison guards would demand a man from each tent come to help push the trucks the last few kilometres to the camp, men who were already exhausted by their relentless labouring. As a sergeant, it was my father's task to choose which man from his tent went. He always chose himself.

King Rat was, I only discovered many years later, written by an Australian named James Clavell who had been a POW in Changi. Clavell's tale was published after a postwar career in English and then American movies. Written during a Hollywood writers' strike in 1960 it seems to have been composed with a keen eye for an American market and sensibility and was an immediate bestseller. Perhaps it was Clavell's experience, or perhaps it wasn't, or perhaps he took those parts he felt would meld with American individualism and made of it a great commercial success.

When I asked my father about the story of him choosing a man from his tent to push the trucks of a night and my father choosing himself, he was annoyed. He said the author had it wrong and that the story was untrue. Yet previously he had told me it was a good book, and a reliable one. It was as though something in the story—beyond its veracity or otherwise—offended him deeply.

6

One day my father visited me and he noticed my bookcases. Do you need all these books? he asked. Doesn't the library have them? It was a gently put query as if the bookcases baffled him, which perhaps they did. But it was also in his way an admonishment. Ever since, I have always felt slightly ashamed of my books for I sensed they—and me with them—had somehow disappointed him. I saw them for the first time through his eyes: a vulgar display of possession. When my father died I met a tall African man at his funeral, a recent migrant to Australia. No one in the family knew who he was. He had come to pay his respects, he said. My father had paid his family's power bill for the last five years.

"Money," my father would say, "is like shit. Pile it up and it stinks. Spread it around and you can grow things."

When as a child I petitioned my parents to let me have a newspaper run like other kids, they demurred. I heard them talking—my mother, my grandmother, my father. They disliked the way that cash was claiming even a child. For them it bordered on offensive. That a child might work was one thing—but money, money they saw as a force that was inherently outside of human control, a force that sought to subjugate everyone it met. Any relationship that became a transaction founded on money was to be mistrusted, as were people who did things for money, who acted only for money, who set the needs of money above the needs of life.

My parents were frugal not simply because they had to be careful, but because they saw little reason for making life about money. The notion of any relationship being what is now termed *transactional,* the idea of *monetising* aspects of your very life, would have seemed to them like some sort of emotional sickness or mental illness.

Along with money, ambition was seen to be dangerous. My mother hoped I would make a *good* plumber. It was that sort of world. Not an excellent plumber or a successful plumber, both adjectives implying some sort of excess of pride, or presumption, that might rend the all-consuming ties of family and duty or destroy a life with the hubris it might invoke. Work was a means, careers were something Americans talked about. Freed of ambition or expectation I was free to do whatever I wished.

I don't mean to suggest that they were stupid about money. Money was good, as the old joke ran, if only for financial reasons. It was an aspect of the world but not the point of it. They were realists, not idealists. "You don't need possessions," my father once said, "but you do need whitegoods that work." They didn't confuse money with life or wish for it to become life.

Near the end of his time, my father, who liked keeping some cash at hand in an envelope in his desk drawer, realised money was routinely going missing. He suspected a young woman who came to clean. Believing she had more need of it than him, he made no attempt to hide the envelope and once a week had my sister refresh its contents.

7

Perhaps at the heart of it all was a fear that came out of something far older. Tasmania was full of the descendants of machine breakers, swing labourers, Luddites, Chartists, trade unionists, slave revolt leaders and Māori chieftans exiled to Van Diemen's Land, as the island was known, the gulag of the British Empire—people united in their various failed efforts to give shape to the revolt against the enclosing capitalism reshaping the world and them with it.

My grandmother on my mother's side, known to all as Mate, once told me of how in her childhood the old people would talk of Ireland during the Famine and how they had witnessed the men of English absentee landlords evicting tenant farmers and their families and burning their homes down in front of them. The story seemed unrelated to our family; she was proud to the point of insistence that she was descended from free settlers and not convicts.

Yet one day she began telling me about the man traps that were set for the escaping convicts; her grandfather had seen them in his work as a constable. She spoke with a surprising lack of elaboration about his experience as a policeman, elaboration normally her way. But no, her memory was solely of the cruelty of a man trap, a giant sort of rabbit trap, a gaping shark's mouth of two iron-teethed jaws rising to thigh height hidden in the bush along the routes favoured by escaping convicts. Covered with bracken and tree litter, the man trap would snap shut when its tensed iron was sprung, ripping through the thigh or calf of the convict as if it were no more than a poor rabbit's leg, tearing flesh apart and crushing bone. The victim would lie in agony until found, sometimes dead, sometimes alive, destined to live as a cripple or to die of infection.

Undone by emotion, Mate said that her grandfather had once discovered a man caught in a man trap *down the peninsula* and her eyes teared up. Emotional display was not Mate's way: even as a child it struck me as unusual.

Her grandfather's name was Edward Green. She knew him as a child. Mate was ashamed of Mad Ned, as she called him. She said he used bad language and was vulgar. Near the end of her life Mate told me that she thought Mad Ned was possibly a convict. On checking the archival record it was discovered that he never had been a constable. He had been a convict, found guilty along with three others of beating a man with a stick in Westmeath, Ireland, and transported to Van Diemen's Land for life. Irish papers of the time reported that he and three others had been transported for being Whiteboys.

The Whiteboys was a secret sect whose members would of a night whiten their faces, don white blouses and ride out to defend the rural poor from enclosure, tithes, low wages and evictions, burning out landlords and occasionally killing them and policemen. Their violence had consequences, limiting the worst excesses of absentee landlordism. But it also met with considerable state violence. Acts were passed to ban the Whiteboys and they were brutally repressed, many being hanged.[4]

When presented with this information Mate stiffened. She denied all knowledge and said it couldn't be so and that he never was. Her mind had clearly been wandering, she said, when she had told me such things.

There is no fineness in violence; it metastasises and spreads. And in my family it was passed down through my grandmother, who was for a time cruel, and through some of her sisters, who were notorious for beating their children for no reason.

And I thought back then on how when Mate had told me the story of the man trap she had started crying about the cruelty of it, perhaps perplexed by what life was and the long shadows that still shaped her, by the questions she could not resolve, while I, an eleven-year-old both bewildered and alert to something I could not yet understand, kept staring at my grandmother who never cried.

8

Years later an aged family relative, Aunty Blossom, described Mate's family coming into the village of Sorell in their dray and the baker's children walking behind chanting "*Crawlers . . . crawlers*."

Crawler. The old convict word for a convict.

Mate's aged brothers and sisters would sometimes arrive at our home and the talk would be of the landed families as if we were one when in reality we were nothing. Great-uncle Babes, who used to play the piano in Ma Dwyer's celebrated Salamanca brothel, the Blue House, would talk of them, the true free settlers—the V—s and the B—s and the C—s, the idiot issue of the English gentry gifted the kangaroo hunting plains stolen from the massacred Aboriginal people for their immense sheep farms along with the gangs of convict slave labourers to work them and make the free settlers obscenely rich—as though they were personal friends when, as one of my brothers observed, they wouldn't have pissed on us if we were on fire.

On this point Blossom was interesting: Mate's family had to invent themselves, she told me. What else could they do? I *admired* them, Blossom said. They were nothing and so they had to pretend to be something until they were.

As she was dying Mate had recurrent dreams of the dray coming to her across the fields and on it were all the old people asking her to come with them. My mother, who loyally sat with Mate those last long weeks, urged her to go with them. But Mate would not. Every night they returned, and now the drayman was a fine-looking young man whom she recognised as Tom, my elder sister's son, not yet eight months old but on the dray he was grown-up and handsome. Finally Mate went away with Tom and the dray. Two weeks after Mate's death Tom died of Sudden Infant Death Syndrome.

9

Mate sat in the dray, eyes averted from the dust kicking up behind it and the baker's children running alongside. She sat in the dray, she sits in the dray, and even now, long after her death, she is sitting there still, straight, looking past them and towards the future, reinventing herself by reinventing her past, not knowing the past stays with us, that what was, is and shall be, as the bakers' children's chant, *Crawlers . . . crawlers,* through time and space haunting her and haunting Tom and haunting us all, unable to be unheard: *Crawlers . . . crawlers . . . crawlers.*

10

Mate was meant to die in 1956 when she had a severe stroke. It was said everyone in our large clan prayed for her to survive, back when she seemed so old but was only middle-aged, younger than me writing this now, that it was a miracle she lived, but perhaps it would have been better, my father later said, if we hadn't prayed. He was unsure about God but sure about prayer, about the power of communal wishing. Yes, he said, perhaps it would have been better for her if she had died back then. That was her time. The rest was just waiting, forty years of it. It would have been better for her to have died, but she didn't or wouldn't, as if some shared love that was also perhaps some insidious vengeance, some dark thing that was love and also wasn't, kept her soul here.

She lied about her age until the end, saying she was ninety-eight and not ninety-nine, to keep the long-lost shame from rising back up, to cover up the sin of having conceived out of wedlock by muddling her age; she would have got the telegram from the Queen and claimed the palace had it wrong, but perhaps to save herself the argument she died and so many years after I still think of her.

Near the end, she moved into a nursing home where she shared a room with Mrs. B—. I never learnt her first name. She was an even smaller woman than Mate, with a round face and eyes that bulged, always smiling, a smile so permanent the rest of her face had slowly fallen into place around it, like a mildewy tent sagging on broken poles.

Mate became fast friends with Mrs. B—, and then Mrs. B— died and another woman took her bed across from my grandmother and Mate made friends with her too, and she died, and another woman came, and this time Mate didn't bother making friends with her because they all died, death was the rule, friends were about living. Mate had the survivor's curse.

At some point her sisters and brothers began dying also, her sisters and brothers the only ones who understood the absurdity of her life and their lives and the only ones I ever saw her laugh with, they all died and she was doomed to outlive two of her sons and most of her siblings, they all died and they were all waiting to die. Perhaps she wondered why God had answered their prayers that she might live when she had her stroke in 1956. Was it God's punishment? Because they all kept dying and she kept living.

Perhaps that was what she thought in her heart of hearts, because the closer she came to death the more I sometimes think she feared God saw everything about her, that God had chosen her out of all the others to punish with life, until even that bedroom was no refuge.

11

I see Mate, red tartan mohair shawl draped over her bony shoulders, day after year after decade playing Patience on her bed table, a weary piece of musk-coloured Masonite with worn wood borders and dulling steel tube legs.

Her smell—an amalgam of ammonia, cheap scent, the soap of her hard scrubbed flesh and the naphthalene of her carefully preserved clothes—repelled me, as she did each morning when she would make her way to the toilet on her stick-like legs, hunched like an aged plover, bearing the chamberpot she kept under her bed, a towel over its indignity. Above all, I silently resented the way she lorded it over our poor mother.

Yet I was Mate's favourite. I don't know why. It was clear that religion, which in her old age mattered greatly, was of no interest to me. Nor was I a remarkable child in any sense. Among her numerous grandchildren—I have over fifty first cousins—many were far more vivacious, attractive, charming, clever, athletic and interesting. But when she told me things I listened.

Each morning one or another of us would have to run breakfast into her bedroom—she was the only person in the house allowed their own bedroom—and put on that bed table her tiny one-cup aluminium teapot with its faux hammer-beaten belly and anodised blue lid, along with a plate of toast: two slices, pale but not anaemic, warm but not cold, and no trace of charring tolerated. These were tight parameters to achieve success within on a busy morning. For any misdemeanours the little hand bell kept next to her bed on a chest of drawers would be heard to tinkle, and in the kitchen remnant grandchildren would look away or scarper, hoping not to be singled out by our mother and told to go see what Mate wanted.

In her bed, propped up on pillows, Mate would sit, bony shoulders shawled, proffering the plate with two uneaten or slightly gnawed pieces of toast along with the curt dismissal: tell Helen the toast was a bit punky. Or: tell Helen the toast was burnt. Our mother was her mother's servant.

We would take the toast back down the narrow dark corridor to the kitchen and our mother. Mate says it's punky. Our mother would then give the cold toast to us to eat or eat it herself and make some more. I refused to eat Mate's toast, to swallow some essential indignity that I couldn't understand.

The whole absurd edifice of Mate's authority and, allied with it and contingent on it, the Church's ludicrous power and sanctity over every aspect of our lives, rested finally with our father's acceptance of both. Only as an adult did it occur to us what Mate was: a widow, a single, penniless, powerless woman, who was to outlive her husband by almost half a century, still receiving letters to her end addressed to Mrs. Jack L—, condemned to surviving on her children's charity. In my mother's case that charity was, in the way of those times, necessarily founded on the agreement of our family's sole breadwinner, our father, and in the hierarchy of the times, its head. And through the decades she lived with us, I never once heard him speak of her with anything other than complete respect.

12

And yet when we went to church, the essence of everything Mate respected, we always sat near the back, the place I seek out to this day at any event, a place where disrespect and comedy flourish, where the power and authority on the stage called the altar are mocked with whispered asides, jokes, mimicry; where one is always closest to the exit and the real world of sun, sea, of life itself. When it came time for Communion, the theatrical catharsis of the mass, I never saw my father partake.

As a child this act of revolt felt powerful and unnecessarily nonconformist. The point of mass was mutual agreement—that much was clear even to a child—and any act of disagreement threatened to upset the whole edifice. Yet there he was, week after week, at church, sitting up in the last few rows and refusing at the apotheosis of the ceremony to agree. He didn't disagree, or say no. He *was* no, the embodiment of no, the most powerful no there is: peaceful, passive, respectfully and adamantly no.

Only now can I see how he said no to almost everything that life offered, not in rage or terror, not with vehemence or in indignation, but with a wry smile and a funny story, amused by the absurdity of the world. His revolt was self-contained and self-sustained. I don't know how he did it.

We justified sitting up the back because the fervour of those who sat up front was seen by us to be undignified, unseemly and ill-judged, their belief too total and too complete. The front of the church was where converts always sat—or so the wisdom of the family had it—and converts were said to be ferocious in their belief.

When I find myself at this other end of life once more sitting up the back of literary and artistic events of today that so resemble the churches of yesterday, old rituals in new drag, with their unquestioning subservience to new orthodoxies and their contempt for difference which many find comforting, replete with their savage castings-out and swooning agreements which many find necessary, my mind drifts. A world of sacrosanct orthodoxy is a world in which the novel and the novelist have no home. A writer, if they are doing their job properly, is always a heretic. As I sit silently through the stale tedium, the po-faced hypocrisies and dreary homilies, my mind is escaping once more into dreams of the sea and sun outside.

13

My father said he was a bush Catholic. A priest would come around once or twice a year to remote places like Cleveland and marry and christen whoever needed such formalities observed. Other than that, Catholicism was not much present. My father's own belief, with which he saw no conflict with his Catholicism, was that people returned to this world as kangaroos, wallabies, wombats and birds. Things were mysterious to him and he found that reassuring. Though a teacher, he did not believe or profess any ultimate answers. He felt a deep connection with the people he was descended from and yet about them he knew next to nothing. We were taken to the places they lived in some lesson that was also a quest, some imparting of knowledge that was also a question he couldn't answer. We would stand just down from the railway line, the old Georgian coaching house at our back, staring at the empty block, there in the bush, where once had stood the railway labourer's wooden cottage in which he had been born. There as a child he had filled out his illiterate father's work sheets in the wavering light thrown by a kerosene lantern in their kitchen, oily shadows abruptly darting across the page when a draught blew, and afterwards read aloud to his father the footy results from *The Sporting Globe*.

14

We had two boxes of comics and twopenny westerns we reread every holidays. There were Phantoms, Eagles, Disneys, some Superman and Batman comics. But the favourites were Phantom and the war comics. It wasn't until I was six or seven that one of my brothers mentioned Dad had been a soldier in the war—there was only one war in those days—and, excited, I asked him, using the lingua franca of war comics, how many Japs he had killed.

My father, whose attention was almost impossible to get, who was so remote and so distant, suddenly turned and fixed his gaze on me.

Never, he said with an anger the ferocity of which I can still feel these years later, never ever ask such a question again.

That was all. Yet the sudden intensity of him I had not experienced before and never would again. It was overwhelming. I was at once undone and bewildered.

He didn't seek me out to explain any of it. It was left to me to slowly piece together the knowledge that a war comic was not war, nor yet life; that there was a real world that had to be addressed with the utmost respect and seriousness. My father liked folly and fancy. What he could not tolerate was when they were conflated with life.

Whenever I hear the babble of nonsense with which politicians dress up the horrors of war, I am once more that seven-year-old child, shocked, bewildered and deeply ashamed.

War, my father told me decades later, is the ultimate obscenity.

15

Our father wasn't impractical but he was uninterested in practical things. He took pride in his neatly kept finger-nails, owning a small half-oval leather wallet containing nail scissors, files and assorted manicure tools he had bought after the war and kept until his death. Coming from a labouring family, a successful sportsman in his youth, something of a local champion, and having only just survived being a slave labourer, he felt no need to prove himself physically, had no interest in manual work and made no pretence he did. Nor did he have his idea of masculinity bound up in it; that is, if he had any idea of masculinity. Men amused him but women interested him. He spoke of women seriously, while men, for the most part, were no more than comic relief. He seemed bored by ideas of masculinity, or perhaps he had simply seen what boys playing at men led to and none of it seemed to him worth the candle.

His primary emphasis in all things was on gentleness, kindness and a certain restraint. Sometimes, at our mother's urging, he would throw me or my sister over his knee to punish us when we'd been badly behaved, raise his hand to smack us on our bottoms, and then shudder. Even today I can feel it, the thrumming of my father's body and its gigantic unknown yet understood history vibrating into me, its incommunicable yet clearly communicated meaning. Shuddering and shuddering, until he threw me back on my feet and walked off, while behind him we would ape his shivering and shaking and silently laugh at him.

And he would allow that too, that we, his children, would mock his strength as weakness.

16

Much to our mother's frustration, our father rarely ate with us, his family, claiming he had work to do, preferring to wait until we were done to then emerge and eat alone. He liked to eat and he liked his food to be for a simple palate. My mother had boarded for a time during the war with Miss Joan F—, who was contemporary in her culinary pursuits, and upon being married my mother, seeking to emulate Miss Joan F—'s example, presented my ever more sullen father with meals of meat and four veg. After a few weeks my father was said to have remarked, "Helen, this modern food is all very well—but can we just get back to the meat and three veg?" And so it was ever after, although my mother, who was both an experimentalist and an adventuress, and unreliable in her enthusiasms, did successfully sneak mushrooms in over some decades, claiming they were offal off-cuts.

There was a strong distinction between adult food and children's food, with products like butter and real cheese reserved for my father, along with the eyes of lamb chops, while the kids made do with margarine and dripping, Kraft silver-wrapped cheese, and the fatty tails of lamb chops. My mother took the worst and ate the leftovers: the burnt bits, the fatty bits, the remains. Food was a hierarchy with my father at its apex and my mother at its base. And yet this was not imposed on her by my father, who merely took what he was given. It came out of some far older order of things in which we were all implicated variously and in servitude to which we all paid a price at some point.

And yet, when my mother lost her way with vascular dementia, my father, in his eighties, took up the domestic burden without complaint and with even a certain gusto, cooking, cleaning, and overseeing my mother's growing needs. My mother, in turn, having erratic memory, would sometimes eat both her meal and his, or take his tablets as well as her own, and all this he bore with a gracious humour. His methods and standards were not necessarily of the first order, but they worked. When one day I visited to find a hairdryer blasting into their refrigerator's deep freeze and I thought he too had lost his mind, he merely pointed out how much easier it was to defrost with this method.

17

My father talked rather less than our mother but when he talked he was original. For a long time I was puzzled by his originality: his principal reading was two local newspapers of despairing quality, the *Hobart Mercury* and the *Launceston Examiner.* As he aged he read both ever more assiduously. Laughter and feeling were closely allied in him and he was particularly taken with what people wrote in obituaries. The doggerel of death in its tragicomedy never ceased to amuse and move him.

He found wisdom and meaning in the most mediocre reportage of local sporting events. He was, in short, a very good reader.

Of the many necessary illusions that enable a writer to write, two are paramount—one, the vanity they can write a good book, and the other the conceit that a good book will be read by good readers, people with the insight to recognise what is good within it. But, of course, good readers are as rare as good writers, perhaps even rarer, and most books in consequence find only poor readers. Writers rail against misunderstanding, but poor writers prosper by being misunderstood, some even accidentally elevated into the pantheon of greatness in consequence, the bad clay of their work forever after glazed with the good fortune of brilliant readings. In a similar way my father blessed every court report and obituary notice with the weight of a remarkable life, finding unexpected depths and breadths in the thinnest journalese and kitschest sentiment, the words nothing, the drift of them everything. His kitchen filled daily with insights that belonged to an order other than that of the rags he read. He told one of my brothers that a single In Memoriam column could contain purer feeling than a book of poetry. He didn't need *literature* to essay the universe. His mind only needed the smallest spark.

18

He once told me he never cried during the war, nor did he cry in the months after Thomas Ferebee released the lever over Hiroshima and 60,000 or 80,000 or 140,000 people died and he lived and finally made it back home to Tasmania. Only forty years later when my elder sister's son, Tom, died did a strange transformation take place. He would see a mesh screen in a car's rear window used to shield a baby from direct sunlight and begin to uncontrollably sob. He would see a child's empty stroller at a park and sob. A mention on TV of a missing child or a sentimental song on the radio and he would sob. He would not seek another room or place of privacy to hide his emotion, perhaps because the world was full of the same sadness, the inescapable sadness that was life, that was the shame of his brutally impoverished family that he, the only one of his siblings, was able to escape with a high school education, that was his mother's death of consumption, that was the many friends he witnessed die in the slave labour camps of Thailand and Japan, a sadness that could only be tempered by the love of those close to you, the love they had for you and you for them. But now his grandson was dead and he, a man in his seventies, could not stop crying. His vegetable garden ran wild and then to seed. The only thing that now occupied his time was making compost for which he had no use, cutting up prunings and forking them over and over.

19

Near the end of his life, my father managed to piece together the story of what had befallen a woman who had vanished from his childhood hamlet when he was a boy. But having solved the mystery he discovered it was just another story, that there was no one left other than himself for whom it was of interest.

And this made my father sad.

"There's no one left to tell," he said.

By which he meant no one for whom it would help, no one for whom it might answer some implacable, inexorable question at the centre of their being. For memories too have their moment. There is a time for forgetting and a time for remembering and then even that time becomes a memory and, after a further time, nothing at all.

20

I knew my father was dying at that moment he told me he loved me. It was the first time he had ever said such a thing. He was ninety-eight. Ironically, one of my earliest memories and enduring terrors was that he would soon die. For so long he was a sick man struggling to hold many things together, his job as a country schoolmaster, his growing family, his marriage, his mind and his body.

He would spend the first week of his Christmas holidays mostly sleeping in that little bedroom with its row of south-facing louvred windows that rattled in the night wind and filled with a soft light in the early morning as the sunrise slowly slanted its way around. We children were warned by our mother not to disturb him. He would be exhausted and said and did little.

At some point he might rise and take us across the track that passed for a road through the mostly empty camping ground—a few tent spots cut into the boobialla linked by more tracks—over the dune and onto the beach. He would carry a folding sun lounge threaded with yellow plastic tubing under one arm and an umbrella across the other shoulder, set himself up, pull his giggle hat over his eyes and go back to sleep, yet keeping, I imagine, more of an eye on us than we thought. Or there again, perhaps not.

The sun would grow in its bite, the ocean would go its very long way out or make its very long way in and we would swim and play, but my father only rarely joined us. He was a family man who liked being alone, a solitary man who nevertheless greatly enjoyed company.

He would lie there in the summer heat, turning so dark that when we went on a family camping trip to the mainland he would be refused service in bars and bottle shops as another half-caste, and each time this happened he never argued or complained or said he was not one of those down on the riverbanks by the country towns we passed through, sitting in circles under the shade of eucalypts under one more of which my father now lies, as he wished, facing northwest where the sun sets on the mountain each evening, buried next to my mother.

That's life.

Three

1

Rebecca West and H. G. Wells were completely wrong for each other, they were completely right; she saw he wouldn't leave his wife, he saw she needed a wife; they jarred each other and annoyed each other from the beginning and from the beginning they were inextricably physically attracted to each other. He thought love was just common sense, she thought it was a way of losing it, he was for sex without love, she was for the whole damn business. He believed he was reinventing literature as a form of proselytising journalism, while she wrote many years after their affair ended, as if still arguing with him, that art was "not a plaything, but a necessity, and its essence, form, is not a decorative adjustment, but a cup into which life can be poured and lifted to the lips and be tasted," and the book she wrote those words in, *Black Lamb and Grey Falcon,* reinvented journalism as literature, prefiguring much of what literature would become.

They should never have met, they were destined for each other, he would make her life and destroy her life and she would make her life in spite of his life, he would be an inexhaustible source of love and friendship for her for the next thirty-five years, he would madden her, he would win her and lose her and win her, she would be the one person he cared to see to the end, and to her immense surprise only after his death would she discover within herself the one thing she had never expected: a crack in the cup of life that opened into a desolation that was utter and inconsolable.

2

Perhaps because she was irresistible Wells at first resisted her. Perhaps he sensed he had met someone his equal—or even greater. In any case, something startled Wells, even frightened him, for he abruptly retreated, and after they had kissed in front of his bookcase, he wanted no more to do with her. He packed up his papers and fled to Switzerland, where he hoped he might escape the confused feelings enveloping him and find a renewed clarity and purity of thought in the spectral whiteness that surrounded Château Soleil, Elizabeth von Arnim's alpine retreat.

3

Rebecca West, though, was not for defeat. For her, love and victory were synonyms. And she was not one for losing. She coupled audacity and ambition with an idea of stability she would forever after mistake older men as offering. She held herself to a high standard. She had written only a few months earlier how unrequited love was pathetic and undignified, adding as proof her contention that Christianity lacked dignity—and by implication was pathetic—not because Christ was crucified, but because his love for the world was unrequited. "A passion that fails to inspire passion," she wrote, "is defeated in the main object of its being."[5]

Having dispensed with God, she wrote to Wells that she was going to kill herself after being rejected by him, that all she could do was love. She had tried to hack the overwhelming love she felt for him back to the little thing he seemed to want. But even that, she realised, was too much for him.

4

Wells arrived at his mistress's magnificent Swiss retreat with his two sons and half a suitcase of scientific reprints concerning the recent discoveries about radium—discoveries that, he told Little e, as he called the diminutive Elizabeth, pleasantly took his mind as far away as laudanum once had Samuel Taylor Coleridge's and which would form the basis of the novel he would write—the story of man summoning a power equivalent to the sun.

And this, no less, Little e said, to be created in our own magnificent house of the sun, Château Soleil!

Wells coughed. The plural pronoun had the effect of entropy on his spirits. He suggested a walk.

After an hour of wandering the Swiss forest, Wells and Little e stopped. While resting, Wells divided between them a copy of *The Times* he had with him. They began reading aloud to each other gobbets of advertisements and articles that amused them. Little e came upon a letter by Mrs. Humphry Ward. She read it in a grim, quivering Victorian falsetto that amused them both, as Mrs. Humphry Ward, the greatest woman writer of the older generation, denounced the moral tone of the younger generation, citing a rising young writer as a most pernicious example of all that was wrong: Rebecca West.

"We decided we had to do something about it," Wells recalled many years later. "So we stripped ourselves under the trees as though there was no one else in the world but ourselves and made love all over Mrs. Humphry Ward."

When they had dressed again, Wells struck a lucifer off his boot and set alight Mrs. Humphry Ward's denunciation of Rebecca West, seeking to exorcise it all in the chill alpine air.

"We burnt her," Wells recalled many years later. "*The Times* flared indignantly, and subsided and wriggled burning and went black and brittle and broke into fragments that flew away."

5

Burning remained on his mind when he sat down the following morning in Château Soleil at a bowed Biedermeier desk. In its cupped middle was the beginnings of his new novel while at the far left side was a neat pile of various research papers and books. Wells was particularly taken with *The Interpretation of Radium* by Frederick Soddy, whose pioneering work with Ernest Rutherford on atomic physics would later win him a Nobel Prize. Wells returned to the page that had made such an impression when the gypsy girl in the blue silk hobble skirt had exploded into his life. The limitless energy that existed in radioactivity, Soddy argued, would, once harnessed, lead to a new world that could "rejuvenate itself perennially." A self-renewing form of energy was the opposite of entropy, the idea of the inevitable running down of all life as energy itself runs out.

Entropy had been the flywheel of Wells's most admired writing; it was entropy, after all, which had given his readers the mesmerising penultimate chapter of *The Time Machine* when the time traveller arrives on a forsaken beach that exists in a perennial brooding twilight at the Earth's endpoint on which the only life forms left are giant algae-slimed crabs. A "sense of abominable desolation" hangs over this world in which the sun is sputtering out, a dying star. In Wells's imaginings Darwinian evolution has been trumped by physics.

But Soddy's book made clear that a destiny imposed on the Earth by entropy was vanquished by the promise of the infinite energy implicit in the atom. In words that Wells would have recognised as a summary of his own most successful fiction, Soddy argued that astonishing new discoveries meant "We are no longer merely the dying inhabitants of a world itself slowly dying."[6]

Decades later, in a preface to a new edition of his "dear old *Time Machine,*" Wells reflected that "the geologist and astronomers of the time told us dreadful lies about the inevitable 'freezing' up of the world—and of life and mankind with it. There was no escape, it seemed." But new scientific discoveries meant that "man will be able to do anything and go anywhere."

It was Soddy's vision of eternal energy that opened a vista of hope for Wells, which he would explore for the rest of his life. Eternal energy chimed better with the circumstances of a globally successful writer in his glamorous mistress's Swiss chalet for whom the world grew a little larger with each passing day. His life was now very far from that of the struggling young writer, with a wife and their two baby children to support, who had written his great visionary works of a dying world in a dark little rented house next to a noisy railway line in Woking.

Wells's early masterpieces had been fantastic nightmares that were all the more effective for refusing to trade in a fantastic style. They slyly coupled a fear of where scientific knowledge might lead to a vertiginous terror of a class-bound hierarchy, a person's precarious foothold on which was only ever an accident away from being lost and them with it, falling, as Wells's family had done when his father, a professional cricketer, had fractured his thigh. The family's principal source of income disappeared and his mother was compelled into domestic service. But by 1912, Wells's name made, his success assured, his ascent complete and his fall a seeming impossibility, he was trading more in dreams of a future where wise men—mostly self-elected scientists—ruled a better world benignly.

Now he and Little e broke beds in the remote alpine inns they frequented on their walks, they made love in alpine forests, rutting like animals in beds of pine needles, and of a night, when she so chose, his chalet bedroom. She had built a secret door from her room that opened into a wardrobe in his through which she would visit. The limits to life he had assumed in his Woking days no longer existed, the forces that had once threatened to drag him back down to the poverty of his childhood were no more, and the idea of entropy and the terror it brought on in him, which had fired his greatest works, was an illusion. Now he lived in a world of perpetual energy. He lifted a sheet for Little e and was grateful the darkness hid his forced smile as the black rain of a still far-off explosion began killing something in his heart.

6

Meanwhile, Rebecca West was writing of how she couldn't conceive of a person who ran about lighting bonfires but feared the flame. Yet that was H.G. He wanted people, she sensed, to quarrel and play with, people who raged and wept. But he did not want someone like her, who burnt.

While Wells's world filled with infinite life, Rebecca West's thoughts were otherwise. To not have him was for her an emotional failure so complete death seemed less. "During the next few days I shall either put a bullet through my head or commit something more shattering to myself than death," she wrote.

> . . . I don't understand why you wanted me three months ago and don't want me now . . . You've literally ruined me. I'm burned down to my foundations . . .
>
> You once found my willingness to love you a beautiful and courageous thing. I still think it was. Your spinsterishness makes you feel that a woman desperately and hopelessly in love with a man is an indecent spectacle and a reversal of the natural order of things. But you should have been too fine to feel like that.

I would give my whole life to feel your arms round me again.

I wish you had loved me. I wish you liked me.

Yours,

Rebecca

P.S. Don't leave me utterly alone. If I live write to me now and then. You like me enough for that. At least I pretend to myself you do.

Wells, having discovered a world of infinite possibility, redoubled his rebuff—though not without leaving the door a little ajar.

"How can I be your friend to this accompaniment?" he replied. "I don't see that I can be of any use or help to you at all. You have my entire sympathy—but until we can meet on a reasonable basis—Goodbye."[7]

7

Wells returned to his new book, beginning not with radium but with fire, commencing—and continuing for perhaps too many pages—like a spirited, if slightly unconvincing Mechanics Institute lecture on mankind's slowly growing mastery of fire as a system of energy out of which civilisation grows. The book Wells now wrote between breaking tavern beds, defiling Mrs. Humphry Ward's thoughts, startling alpine deer and trying not to think of Rebecca West, was, it is not unjust to suggest, confused.

Wells later blamed Little e for a loss at this time of his ability to concentrate on the higher needs of his craft and of his artistic focus. Perhaps though the confusion of Wells's new novel mirrored the confusion of the life of a man with a wife and a mistress now feeling the gravitational pull of a third woman he desperately wishes to exorcise from his panicked soul as again he hears the low rumble of the hidden door in his wardrobe sliding open.

But Rebecca West was not for exorcising.

And at such times he wanted to destroy all that he had with Little e, except for the fact it was everything he craved—sex, security, discretion, an amusing, talented, interesting woman.

But it was not Rebecca West.

He found Rebecca disturbed—and disturbing. But much as he tried to burn her to ash it was that wild flame he coveted.

Wells was no product of a twenty-first-century American writing school instructed to only show and never tell when writing their tales. His global success was built on showing *and* telling, and when a new thought came upon him at the writing table, telling some more. Borges's observation that Wells was interested in everything except the story he was writing was never truer than in what was to be published as *The World Set Free*.

In his new book, characters only slouched out of the shadows occasionally and none was a protagonist of sufficient gravity to interfere with Wells's numerous swerves off page. None seemed anything other than a cipher to advance arguments and opinions. His principal belief was that human beings, when confronted with the existential horrors that would arise in consequence of modern scientific discovery, would react rationally, and form a rational world government that would work rationally towards rationally ending the world of its irrational problems.

Where his early nightmares had been taut, these later dreams bloated as his mind went everywhere except the manuscript at hand. Distracted by the pine needles that fell out of his underwear of an evening, unsettled by the spectral vision of a naked Little e appearing unannounced out of his wardrobe like a music hall magician's risqué assistant, disturbed by her warmth and scent that then flowed like a river of wonder into his bed, Wells was undone over and over by the illicit thought of another body that filled his senses whenever Little e filled his arms, that of a hobble-skirted gypsy.

The sound of a distant train came and went. He felt that something in his life was askew but necessary, that same thing which demanded he destroy what he needed. Something delightful had come into his life and this thought he experienced as two fragrant arms around his neck. As his senses swam in lavender the world seemed very agreeable to him. All that lay before him was suddenly clear and straightforward. What was wicked was necessary and yet what was necessary would not end happily or well. He did not care.

He wanted to know life. He did not wish to hide from it. He wondered if the pain that would inevitably flow was somehow as necessary to him as the joy it might bring. And then another distant train sounded and disappeared and he could not return to these thoughts or the lavender smell or understand what a moment before had seemed so clear and straightforward. Everything was once more only the most dreadful tangle as Little e pulled her lips away from his and softly asked him in that voice he had begun to find inexplicably irritating to tell her what he was thinking.

8

Under such trying circumstances, the new book proceeded unevenly. What was meant to bring to the public's attention the revolutionary potential of radium ended tediously with the story of Marcus Karenin, a Russian sage dispensing cod-wisdom at a Himalayan sanatorium where he has gone to die. A poet argues with Karenin that a great awakening of sexual love is taking place, but the Slavic seer will have none of it: in the new enlightened age long life will liberate us all from the demands of sex and allow us to concentrate on higher things. If it was wishful thinking reflecting a personal dilemma rather than a universal truth Wells's pen nevertheless staggered on plumbing the ever more implausible.

After all, hadn't he pulled off similar narrative non sequiturs in some of his earlier books and triumphed? But where once unlikely tropes and strange leaps had succeeded, nothing worked anymore, and Wells knew it. He worried, he confided to Little e, that H. G. Wells was a mad man who thought he was H. G. Wells.

Only once did he touch the place that had led him to his greatest stories. Wells had an unnerving ability to discern the destructive possibilities of embryonic scientific discoveries and new technology. Tanks, aerial warfare, the mass bombardment of civilians and the growing lack of separation between the killing of military personnel and the innocent—all these he had foreseen in his earlier novels. And now, between fire, world history, world government and his forlorn hope that perhaps sex might be better vanquished for all concerned—Little e, Rebecca West, Jane, himself, and humanity—there came to him a nightmare redolent of his greatest works, his most enduring nightmare that he would bequeath to posterity and which would come to forever after hang like the sword of Damocles over the world.

Long before the scientists, far earlier than any generals or politicians, Wells had extrapolated from the work of Rutherford and Soddy a military application of the scientists' discoveries about radium in a new weapon of hitherto unimaginable power. Humanity, Wells wrote, echoing Rebecca West's letters about him, was a "sleeper who handles matches in his sleep and wakes to find himself in flames." Wells's invention was an idea of such depraved monstrosity that it shocked even Little e.

"All you want to do," she told Wells, "is destroy things."

Wells called his invention the atomic bomb.

9

Wells imagined the atomic bomb as an infinitely more destructive force than conventional explosives, a weapon so powerful that a man "could carry about in a handbag an amount of latent energy sufficient to wreck half a city." The idea had been vaguely mooted by a few scientists but it was Wells who first foresaw the monstrous reality and consequences clearly and in detail.

Derived from his scientific understanding of the radical implications of the potential energy in atoms, he imagined in *The World Set Free* the discovery of "artificial radioactivity" in 1933, the subsequent invention of atomic bombs, and an all-out global nuclear war in the 1950s. Wells's atomic bombs are hand-tossed by aviators out of open plane cockpits, the effect no less devastating for the almost comic mode of their delivery.

At the time Wells was writing of the perils of nuclear war, even military planes remained highly experimental creations, at once still ludicrous to behold and largely impractical to use. That summer, the British Military

Aeroplane competition had been won by a Cody V biplane, a fanciful contraption that Little e described, not without justification, as an oversize box kite tacked onto a tricycle. Wells reminded her of the sensational global news of the world's first aerial bombardment in Libya two years before when an Italian aviator tossed four hand grenades, each the size of a grapefruit, on Ottoman forces from an Etrich Taube, a plane the shape of which suggested a confused moth.

The notion of such mechanical absurdities being capable of any serious military role in the age of the mighty dreadnoughts remained, however, an idea only slightly less ridiculous than suggesting the end of civilisation was implicit in the unseeable atom.

10

"I was dumbfounded," the B-29's radar operator, Joe Stiborik, recollected about what he saw happen to Hiroshima after Thomas Ferebee released his lever. "Here was a whole damn town nearly as big as Dallas, one minute all in good shape and the next minute disappeared . . . There was almost no talk I can remember on our trip back to the base. It was just too much to express in words, I guess."

And yet it was words H. G. Wells used thirty-two years before, not only to express what Joe Stiborik was to witness, not only to predict what would happen at Hiroshima, but also to create the very possibility of Hiroshima. Fiction may be only fancy yet reality is often no more than the enthusiastic answer we give to our dreams and nightmares. Wells's words set in train a chain of events—or, to use a more apposite image, set off a chain reaction that led to the mute shock of the bomber's crew as the silver B-29 banked away from the mushroom cloud and the instant death of innumerable people below, some vaporised leaving only their shadow etched into concrete pavements and walls as evidence of having lived, others condemned to a life that would be a death extended over agonising hours, days, weeks and in some cases years and decades.

"My God," the co-pilot, Captain Robert Lewis, said over the intercom, "what have we done?," the meaning of which has been much debated ever since.

11

Wells's atomic bombs are characterised by the paradox of their small size ("a black sphere two feet in diameter") relative to their enormous, hitherto unimaginable destructive power. When the atomic bomb detonates, Wells's aviators observe "a shuddering star of evil splendour" appearing far below, a description unconsciously evoked three decades later by the real-life aviator Captain George Marquardt, who piloted an observation plane that accompanied Thomas Ferebee's B-29 when it dropped the atomic bomb on Hiroshima. "It seemed," he later recalled, "as if the sun had come out of the earth and exploded."

Wells clearly foresaw how the site of an atomic bomb explosion would for "a score of miles in diameter" become "death areas" while "luminous, radio-active vapour" drifting "scores of miles from the bomb centre" would kill all it overtook. Bob Caron, the bomber's tail gunner, saw Hiroshima "being covered with this low, bubbling mass. It looked like bubbling molasses, let's say, spreading out and running up into the foothills, just covering the whole city."

Wells described how the bomb "spread itself out into a monstrous cavern of fiery energy at the base of what became a miniature active volcano . . . a boiling confusion of molten soil and superheated steam," a description eerily close to that made by Thomas Ferebee decades later. "I saw this boiling on the ground and the stem [of the mushroom cloud] was going up and you could see buildings going up in the steam." Bob Caron recalled how the cloud "was white on the outside and it was sort of a purplish black towards the interior, and it had a fiery red core, and it just kept boiling up."

"There was nothing but death in that cloud," the then-twenty-four-year-old assistant flight engineer, Robert Shumard, commented many years later. "All those Japanese souls ascending to Heaven."

12

Yet by the standard of Wells's previous and spectacular successes *The World Set Free* was a failure. The lazy plotting, the tedium of its characters, and Karenin's ramblings failed to win a large audience. Published in 1914 to poor sales and worse reviews, the *Times Literary Supplement* dismissed it as "porridge."

By then Wells's affair with von Arnim was over and Wells and West had become lovers. On 4 August 1914, the same day that the First World War began, their son, Anthony Panther West, was born.

After the war to end all wars—another Wells line that began as an idealistic expression and ended up a cynical catchphrase—Wells and West parted. He ceased writing the great novels for which he would be remembered and began writing books no one any longer recalls that paradoxically made him one of the most famous writers on Earth. Rebecca West became Rebecca West and, finally, many decades later, a version of Mrs. Humphry Ward, defending Senator Joe McCarthy and denouncing *The Times* and parts of the BBC as Communist Party organs. She became somebody who had once been somebody else and then was no more than jetsam that signified something mysterious and slightly incomprehensible, somehow out of reach, lost long ago behind the vast seawall of great wars and passing time.

The World Set Free was forgotten.

13

Yet Wells's novel has a claim on subsequently becoming one of the most influential books of the twentieth century. One aspect gripped a few imaginations. "Trained scientist as he is," the *Scientific American* declared in its review of the novel, "he presents his atomic bomb with an air of definiteness and conclusiveness that almost convinces one it exists."

This definite and conclusive idea of an atomic bomb proved resonant. Slowly it took purchase on influential minds. One was Wells's good friend Winston Churchill, who routinely read all Wells's novels twice. "Might a bomb no bigger than an orange be found to possess a secret power to destroy a whole block of buildings," Churchill asked in an article in the *Pall Mall Gazette* in 1924 tellingly titled "Shall We All Commit Suicide?," "nay to concentrate the force of a thousand tons of cordite and blast a township at a stroke?"

14

"Bomb away!" said Thomas Ferebee and the B-29 bomber his captain, Colonel Paul Tibbets, had named *Enola Gay* after his mother, Enola Gay Tibbets, banked steeply away to escape the blast while in Hiroshima 60,000 or 80,000 or 140,000 people were already dead. The dying, possessed of similar feelings towards their parents as the captain of the *Enola Gay*, were frequently heard to call one word over and over in their final agony, as they wandered lost and blind through the burning ruins of Hiroshima.

Mother, they kept saying as charred skin fell like long strands of kelp off their bodies and heads, *mother.*

Four

1

The past then was different than the past is now; further away and harder to find, it receded more quickly and was little recorded in comparison to today, existing only in archives far away or sometimes not at all. People died younger and memory struggled to see over the great embankments of history—the war, the Depression, the Great War.

And yet the past was also more present. On Anzac Day those who had fought not for Australia but for Tasmania and the British Empire in the Boer War still paraded. Change came slowly and it was possible to conceive of the nineteenth century as a time not unlike now. For a short while yet, people still talked of the arrival of electricity, the shock of the first telephone call and Al Jolson singing, and the exceedingly strange ways Americans were discovered to speak.

My father remembered how the coming of electric light killed ghost stories.

2

When I died on the Franklin River at the age of twenty-one it was as I had always known it would be. Everything ever since has been an astonishing dream. Increasingly, I expect that in my final moments I will wake in the river dark, discovering I never left and am now to drown, and that the only novel I ever wrote was my life.

Perhaps this is a ghost story and the ghost me.

3

I was struck at the death of both my mother and father how within only minutes of passing, their face was no longer them and yet it remained their face. After twenty-one I stole my face back from death but it was not my face. I saw bodies and faces that were me but which I hadn't been allowed, rather this stranger's body and face, like borrowed clothes at once too loose and too tight and smelling wrong. But there was nothing else to wear and so we got on with it, me and this ill-fitting costume that bears my name.

4

It was only many years after it happened that I began to understand. That what occurred is still occurring. I wrote about the story in one way a long time ago for another novel, my first. Though I tried to be honest, it was still happening and so it was dishonest. That's what I couldn't see then that I see now, that though it happened then it's still happening now and it won't ever stop happening, and that writing about it, that writing about anything, can't be an opinion about what happened as if it had already happened when it is still happening, still unintelligible, still mysterious, and all writing is trapped in tenses when life isn't. Life is always happening and has happened and will happen, and the only writing that can have any worth confounds time and stands outside of it, swims with it and flies with it and dives deep within it, seeking the answer to one insistent question: who loves longer?

5

Back when I was writing my first novel, writing being something in which I had no confidence, I was out walking through town one day and bumped into M—, the only writer I knew, a late-middle-aged English woman. When I say a writer, M— was an academic who had one small book of poems slightly larger than a cigarette pack to her credit at that time. But she thought like a writer and believed in writing and was very kind to people like me who wished to be a writer yet didn't have to their name anything so remarkable as a book of poems slightly larger than a cigarette packet.

M— knew of *literature:* she had been to Cambridge in the 1950s where she knew Ted Hughes and Sylvia Plath. This was deeply impressive in 1980s Tasmania. Ted Hughes and Sylvia Plath may as well have been Count Vronsky and Anna Karenina. The idea of them as real people brought on a frisson of wonder in all who listened to M—'s tales. She had been at the infamous *St. Botolph's Review* party where Ted, as M— called him, abandoned his then girlfriend for Sylvia, as M— called her. The teary girlfriend sought solace in M—. Pointing to the new couple engaged in amorous intimacies in a distant dark corner, she sobbed, "Ted has run off with that awful American girl."

"Don't worry," M— replied. "It won't last."

M— asked me what I was doing. I told her I was writing a novel. And when she asked what it was about I told her. Her eyes, moony and watery, dropped to the bitumen pavement as if searching for a lost ring and remained there. Finally she sighed.

"Well, they do say there are only six stories in the world and a dying man is one of them."

She said this ruminatively, which is to say like a cow chewing a cud it would rather not.

I hastily added that it had some other things in it too. I said this unconvincingly, perhaps because I was now unconvinced myself. I hadn't known that what I had lived, was living and would forever live was something so commonplace as to be tedious and not worthy of *literature*.

M—'s first book has some poems I like to this day. The book's page numbering though is a mystery, beginning at page 163 and ending at page 192, as if it is the conclusion to some larger, lost work. Or maybe that's a poem too. It's in fragments that we find ourselves.

The book is called *Tricks of Memory*.

6

There was almost no publicity for my first novel. I did do a spot on a late-night Melbourne radio boxing show because my cousin, Arthur "Mad Dog" Kemp, had been a well-known Melbourne boxer in the late 1960s. Boxing did not feature in my first novel and novels did not feature in late-night Melbourne radio boxing shows as a matter of course. In that interview I talked about Arthur meeting Muhammad Ali when Ali flew into Australia in 1972 and asked to meet some black people. They took him to the Fitzroy Park in Melbourne where Arthur was sitting under a tree sharing a drink with some Aboriginal friends. Arthur recognised the great man, followed by a phalanx of media, walking towards them. Rising unsteadily to his feet Arthur shook Ali's hand.

"You're not the greatest," Arthur said. "I am."

"No," Ali replied, "you're just the ugliest."

A year later, on Christmas Eve, after an afternoon of social drinking, I did a second radio interview about my novel, this time on local Tasmanian radio, and ended up feeling not unlike Cousin Arthur. The interviewer said he'd heard a story about me having once nearly drowned and was it true my novel was based on this experience?

I said, Mmm, and then he asked how I nearly drowned. I said Mmmmm. The sounds weren't exactly Mmm, the sounds were lots of vowels and consonants stacked up, Jenga-like, in growing towers of complex sentences, but at the end of it all they can be summed up as one tall Mmmmm that kept collapsing.

After that I felt a wretched liar, an imposter, a fake.

After that I thought I am never going to talk about it again because to talk about it was only to lie.

7

Words seemed part of the problem, symbols in search of something to symbolise, and all too soon outdated, and some words, old words, no longer made sense. The words from my childhood, unknown today, common then in Tasmania: flogger (a figure of contempt), deadflog (someone who had no spirit and was irredeemably stupid), rummy (strange, odd), rummun (a likeable character), all are convict words. A flogger was originally the flagellator. To be flogged was an experience frequently compared with rape for the psychological and spiritual destruction that flowed from the physical horror. A deadflog was a man broken by flogging. To gammon (to make believe, make up, fantasy)—a word my father remembered as common in his childhood but which I have only heard used by Aboriginal people in far north Australia—was to dream and so escape.

All words are at best transitory and soon enough become archaic, ceasing to belong to language at all and instead becoming the property of data sets that after a further time return only dead URL links, so many 404 errors. In this sense, all words are at best IOUs that if not immediately redeemed fail to deliver on their initial promise. And how long before *data sets, URL, link, 404 errors* and *IOU* also vanish from shared understanding?

Yet words exist to grasp the world and if every day afresh the world eludes them, every tomorrow they are condemned to begin their crazy dance again: words to anchor, the world to fly; words to say it is so, the world to say it is not. And so they tango eternally, words and the world, writers no more than dancing shoes sliding between the dancer and the dance floor.

8

Don't be a crawler, son, my mother would admonish me as a child. A fear, deeply buried, that kept surfacing.

Meaning, don't give in, stand up, be your own person. My father told me how his father, my grandfather, a railway fettler, looked down on the farm labourers on the big sheep farms that abutted the section of railway on which he laboured as a fettler, for he was a proud union man, a free man, while they were *crawlers,* still receiving the old convict ration, as they would until the 1940s, of seven pounds of flour, seven pounds of mutton, and so many ounces of tea and sugar each week, supplemented with the most meagre cash wage.

Starting my first job when I left school, chainman for a surveyor, I listened to David Bowie and the Sex Pistols, but I saved up to buy the *de rigueur* work wear for a labourer—a heavy black wool jacket known as a bluey, the same jacket once issued to convicts. Some workers in the seventies still even wore flannels, the old woollen long-tongued undershirts, peasant wear, convict wear.

There was a great remembering that was also a great forgetting, one hundred years of silence that sounded like a scream the closer you listened. You couldn't be with a girl or the girl with you without being told gossip about their great-grandmother or a distant cousin a century before, and yet of the convicts and Aboriginal people little was ever said. Of a slave system and a genocide nothing. What remained was either silence or lies. Such as: the convicts and their children had all fled to the mainland during the gold rushes. Such as: the Tasmanian Aboriginal people were extinct, long gone, not one left on the island. Such as: everyone was descended from free settlers, not a touch of the tar brush or the convict stain on any of us. And yet when I began work in the 1970s as a labourer, I saved my paltry wages that arrived each week in a small brown envelope to buy a convict coat and dress like the convict I was told I never was.

To be free I had to squeeze the convict blood out of me drop by drop, word by word, book by book.

9

My mother and my father—how much I don't know about them. How much is forever closed to my curiosity, how limited, in any case, is my curiosity. About their secret lives I see not so much closed doors as a child's reticence to open another. But some things are clear. It never occurred to them that they might escape the fate life had decreed for them because destiny was unavoidable; what mattered to them was meeting fate looking it squarely in the eye. My father would quote his brother, my uncle Tom, the possum snarer and later railway yard labourer: "You can sit on me but you can't shit on me."

My father's childhood home, a railway worker's cottage, sat on the railway line that ran through Colonel C—'s vast landholding, originally granted to John Batman, the man whose death squad massacred

Aboriginal people throughout the northeast as he took their land. When Colonel C—'s man burst into my grandmother's kitchen demanding Tom's dog so that he might kill it, claiming it had been killing Colonel C—'s sheep, Tom, who trapped of a night and slept of a day, emerged from his bedroom with his hunting rifle and pointed it at Colonel C—'s man.

"Shoot the dog," he said, "and I'll shoot you."

10

So much of my own life—perhaps the most important parts—are simply blank to me. What remains? Small, beautiful fragments. Me lying as a seven- (or eight- or nine-) year-old with my big sister in long grass in the old abandoned Forth River cemetery amidst half-drunk headstones of long-forgotten family, watching a cloud racing by, summer wind rustling the tall river eucalypts, my head slightly intoxicated by the somehow obscene funk of the thrusting, insistent green growth, a smell stronger than much else so much more substantial about which I can recall nothing. And vanished too whole years that I have been alive.

Capturing an old Clydesdale horse when camping as a twelve-year-old with the Wing brothers up North Motton by a creek we fished for blackfish and lobster, and riding the horse's giant frame bareback, clutching its coarse black neck hair rough as old sisal, waiting for a great fall that never happens, and everyone laughing as they watch. And what remains after all that time is the incomparable joy I felt at that moment, the overwhelming odour and heat and power of the horse, and the race of uncontrollable laughter running between us. It was a time of wonder and all things had the shape of miracles. And like a miracle, no evidence that it ever happened remains.

11

When I try to recall them my family scatters into shards I cannot hold on to but only occasionally dragoon into parts of a story. First one uncle then another was driven off their small mixed farms, both broke, unable any longer *to make a go of it*. A mainlander buys *a hobby farm*. The two ideas seemed to me as a child mutually incompatible. Yet the two ideas are the future.

My eldest brother saw *The Graduate* and said his life had changed. An uncle who spent the Depression living and trapping in a cave in the snow country back of Ben Lomond dies playing darts in the St. Leonards Hotel. My eldest sister sang the chorus to "America" and "I Feel Pretty" from *West Side Story* and shimmied her hips. She and her best friend A— turned up at our shack fresh from teachers' college in Launceston both wearing pedal pushers, tight calf-length slacks that were all the fashion back in some long-ago golden summer. It must have seemed far from where she had been only a few years before when, at the loveless Deloraine convent school she hated, she had been given the first line of the essay her class was to write on Beatlemania: "The Beatles make me ashamed to be a woman."

12

Sometimes they come to me in dreams as they once were, so young, one brother's adolescent beard that will not join for what seems decades but is perhaps months, two wispy mutton chops parted by a small river of downy chin awaiting a final fording. By the time they join into a beard the sixties are over. He is arguing with my parents about the war—the only war, Vietnam—and of course the church, neither of which he agrees with, and walks off. Our elder brother, the most loyal and obedient of us, following his family and the church, his mother and grandmother's Catholic anti-Communist line, supports the war but nevertheless stands up to my parents, arguing that our mutton-chopped brother is allowed to have his opinions. My mother sees his defence as disrespect.

His piercing light blue eyes that struck me even as a child as open to wonder glisten with tears, until there is something shocking about his rage and his sadness, and his inability to communicate what it is that is so upsetting him.

As I watch dumbstruck from afar my mutton-chopped brother tells me he—pointing to our brother—doesn't want to go off to the war he supports. But he'll still go, he says.

The war hung over us. The war hung over everyone then.

I won't go, he continues. I ask what conscription is. He is brooding. I just won't, he says.

I ask again. And when he explains conscription I too become frightened because I understand this much: that our family can now be pulled apart, that the war can take all my brothers, tear them away from us. That they can die.

Later my blue-eyed brother has what might be termed a breakdown. It was, I think now, a crisis of belief. He is some years making himself whole.

In that time he took me camping. He talked to me about the world he was discovering daily. He dreamt of making a kayak and never does. I do. I am not sure why. Perhaps because he made it sound magical, or because I wanted to emulate his spirit of adventure. Perhaps I was enchanted with rivers from the beginning and just needed a boat. Perhaps because when I was eleven, Olegas Truchanas, the celebrated Tasmanian photographer, drowned and the tremor of shock seemed to run through the island. Following the destruction by damming of the exquisite alpine Lake Pedder, Truchanas had returned to kayak the Gordon River and photograph its wonders. He drowned in the river he hoped his images might save from another destruction in another hydroelectric scheme. And then the Gordon was dammed and destroyed too.

It was the first time I ever knew someone die for a belief and the belief was a river, a lake, an idea become a place, and now places, in turn, had become new ideas—of life, of freedom, of hope. One last wild river remained and was to be dammed next, a tributary of the Gordon called the Franklin River, and in turn it became a symbol. At thirteen I made my own kayak, taking the first steps that led to my death at twenty-one, finding myself kayaking not so much rivers as journeying ever deeper into the wonder that first filled my brother's eyes.

13

I phone him to ask why he wanted to build a kayak. He's an old man now. He can't remember anything about his kayak dream. As we talk he recalls a lift home to Rosebery for the holidays sixty years earlier from his Catholic boarding school, later to acquire a notorious name for its roll call of paedophilic priests, that school that hurt so many, with a friend whose father is an old Pole. Heading into Hellyer Gorge the snow begins to fall, softly, then heavily, enveloping the solitary car and its passengers in an otherworldly time and place. He feels it as an embrace, knowing he is soon going to be warm and loved once more. With the old Pole at the wheel, a man who has seen so much, he knows no matter how heavily it snows he is safe.

As an old man he still remembers the freedom and security of being driven through that wildland as the snow continued falling, journeying through its white wonder, homeward bound. Comforted. Amazed. He tells me that an old school friend whose life was destroyed by the sexual abuse he suffered at the school is coming to see him this weekend for the first time since they were children. His friend is dying of cancer.

And then he is talking of the ancient snowing world so many decades before, white-mantled manferns bowing, myrtle leaves shining, a beauty that as an old man he understands as the goodness of this world welcoming him safely home.

Five

1

Water was for Leo Szilard both a terror and a blessing. Even the indolent waters of Oxford's Isis frightened him. When invited, he refused to go punting with a girl there. Unable to overcome his childhood terror of the violent cataract of water that erupted from the nineteenth-century cast-iron water closets of Budapest, he would forever after refuse to pull the chain or empty his baths. These habits, less than endearing, led to his eviction from his rooms at the University of Chicago's Quadrangle Club in 1945, while later saving his life when an oncologist using the toilet after him saw blood and diagnosed bladder cancer. He would prescribe his own radiation treatment and be cured, but of the strange polarity of his intense emotion about water there was to be no cure.

For Leo Szilard perversely loved baths.

And on a long-ago morning in the Imperial Hotel, Russell Square, which boasted its variety of baths and hydropathic devices—from Russian vapour baths to Turkish baths to Aix and Vichy douches—as the very finest and most comprehensive in London, a naked Szilard stood watching as water flowed, steam rose and the tub filled below his garlic bulb torso—plump, portly disarray even at his young age. It was 12 September 1933. There was nothing portentous whatsoever about one more London day that was overcast, grey and drizzling. The Hungarian-Jewish refugee recently fled from Nazi Germany continued staring downwards, lost in thought, flaring his nostrils to better inhale the soothing steam.

2

His girlfriend had left him to work with the poor in India. He was jobless. He was so wretched with a head cold that the day before, he had abandoned his plan to train to Leicester, dashing his hope of hearing speak there the man who while working with Frederick Soddy had famously first divined the mysteries of the atom, the Nobel laureate and the most famous scientist in the land, Lord Ernest Rutherford.

Leo Szilard was too a sort of scientist, but one of an independent cast. He felt his talents were not always helped by the torpor and ardour of a laboratory. His favoured method of scientific research had at its apex the habit of long walks and longer baths, baths necessarily replete with daydreaming reveries, baths so long that a chambermaid once thought he had drowned. It was said that ideas flowed from him as water from a fountain. Certainly it was immersed in water that Leo Szilard felt he had his best ideas. Many years later he would write a story in which dolphins with minds like his, and an irrational belief in the power of rationality like his, remade the world as a peaceful place. He lowered his doughy body into the tub. As he sank back into the hot water it felt, as it always did, that water was his true, natural medium.

3

In his fictions Leo Szilard's great influence was his favourite novelist, H. G. Wells, who bowed not before the dark and irrational but looked towards the hope of science and the light of reason to liberate the world.

George Orwell believed that up until 1914 Wells was "a true prophet." "Thinking people who were born at the beginning of the century are in some sense Wells' own creation," he wrote in a 1941 essay on Wells's legacy that could just as well have been written about Leo Szilard's destiny. "The minds of all of us, and therefore the physical world, would be perceptibly different if Wells had never existed."

If Wells was the prophet, Leo Szilard had for some years prior to his bath in the Imperial Hotel been a disciple, attracted both to Wells's scientific prophecies as well as to his vision of a "new world order" (a typically sweeping and enduring Wellsian trope that equally typically came to mean the opposite of what he intended) based on rational thought and led by scientists and intellectuals.

While visiting London in 1929, Szilard met Wells at a London dinner. The young Szilard, as enchanted with Wells as the young Rebecca West had once been, returned to Berlin where he threw himself into making real the idea of a Wellsian intellectual and scientific elite that would, over some generations, help guide German society to a better place. For a time he even had a small coterie of followers—whom he called the Bund—involved in the idea.

When asked his opinion of Szilard and his Bund, Albert Einstein replied that Szilard was "a genuinely intelligent man, not generally inclined to fall for illusions. Perhaps, like so many such people, he tends to overestimate the role of rational thought in human life."

Einstein and Szilard were friends, and together invented a refrigerator without mechanical parts to help the poor. They first met in 1920 when Szilard moved to Germany after being thrown down a set of steps leading to the Budapest University by anti-Semites and realising that it was time to leave Hungary. An outstanding student, Szilard had trained as an engineer, but in Berlin, the epicentre of modern physics, he pursued the new science.

4

It was later said that in Berlin he had walked with gods. He certainly had no issue with arguing with the immortals he met along the way. On meeting Max Planck, Germany's greatest physicist and a Nobel laureate, in the year Szilard arrived, the unknown twenty-two-year-old student announced, "I only want to know the facts of physics. The theories I will make up."

In the very first class he took with Einstein, Szilard had the temerity to challenge the great man on a matter of physics that led Einstein to reconsider and finally agree with his young usurper. Within two years of arriving, he had a doctorate from the University of Berlin. Einstein had at first listened in disbelief to his young student presenting his thesis on the second law of thermodynamics before grasping the ideas Szilard had formed in baths and over long walks. A second paper on thermodynamics, written six months after his doctorate, was to prove a key influence decades later in the development of information theory. Erwin Schrödinger, the inventor of wave dynamics and no slouch when it came to profundity and originality, wrote that Szilard "was always profound and original."

He was also lazy, charmed many and frequently irritated more. Even then he was mysterious, mercurial and impossible to pin down in time or space, simultaneously in this country or the next, patenting seemingly odd inventions such as linear accelerators and cyclotrons—devices that would allow physicists to further study the atomic nucleus—and coming up with ideas for everything from electron microscopes to a Wellsian new world order over coffee and cake at the Romanisches Café while discussing the quantum mechanics of Heisenberg or the growing political chaos engulfing the Weimar Republic.

Leo Szilard believed that in science the greatest thoughts are the simplest. Yet his abilities sometimes seemed more mystical than rational. He embraced unlikely connections and implausible paradoxes, combining contradictory instincts with an almost eerie prophetic gift, predicting at the Great War's outset the collapse of the German, Russian and Austro-Hungarian empires. He was sixteen.

And so when Hitler was made German chancellor in January 1933 Leo Szilard once more foresaw Europe's fate at a time when many others could not. His desperate entreaties to his friends and family to leave before it was too late were for the most part ignored. He fled Germany in March 1933 and, several months later, in the Imperial's dining room, over a cup of risible English coffee, breakfasting on several spoons of orange marmalade while reading *The Times,* his dreaming eyes alighted on something that interested him more than several depressing articles about the current world situation: a report of the lecture he had missed in Leicester the day before.

Owlish face expressionless, he absentmindedly alternated sips of coffee with spoons of the sticky orange rind as he read how Lord Rutherford, discussing the recent success of two British scientists in splitting the atom through particle bombardment, dismissed any talk of such discoveries leading to "the release of atomic energy on an industrial scale" as "moonshine."

Szilard knew Rutherford was in good company in his conclusion. Both Niels Bohr and Einstein regarded particle bombardment as scientifically important but practically useless. A hugely inefficient process, it took vastly more energy to split the atom than the energy that was released in consequence. Had not Einstein himself compared particle bombardment with "shooting birds in the dark in a country where there are only a few birds"? The analogy accorded with the known facts, thought Leo Szilard. But what about all that was unknown?

5

As steam played over the bath waters, his heavy head full of contradictory thoughts he needed to tease out, Leo Szilard found it pleasant to let his ideas off the leash. In this way he passed some hours, a bespectacled porpoise surfing in the wake of others. Rutherford was undoubtedly an expert. But what was an expert? Someone focused on what little was known and not the much greater sum of what wasn't? Someone who knew only what could not be done but not what might be possible? But then these ideas drifted away with the wisps and drifts of steam wafting around his hairy waist until snagging on a memory: a novel by Wells he had read the previous year. The title escaped him. There were so many books and pamphlets by Wells that it was hard to remember even a fraction of the ones he had read. It was not well known. What *was* it called? He recalled that he had experienced that strange excitement of a reader who has accidentally stumbled into what feels like the deeper, private recesses of a favoured author's mind, almost a frisson of intimacy.

And then he remembered.

The World Set Free.

Abruptly his mind filled with visions of mass atomic war in all its horror: a world in flames, cities boiling, millions killed. Wells's visions, formed in his flight from love. His thoughts scudded this way and that, a welcome sweat broke out on his forehead. *The World Set Free*—a book about what wasn't known that nevertheless revealed just what the liberation of atomic energy on a large scale might mean.

What if Rutherford were wrong?

As he lay back in his tub that autumnal London morning, Leo Szilard wondered why the forecasts of writers sometimes prove to be more accurate than those of scientists. Admittedly he had done little work in atomic physics. This struck him as an advantage. He was unburdened by knowing things. *The theories he could make up.* He told himself that science was above all a product of the subconscious. The creative scientist, he felt, had much in common with the artist and the poet.

His mind slid off with the bath mist into other things—the work he was doing helping other refugee scientists fleeing Nazism, moonshine, his girlfriend, masturbation, particle bombardment and pilots gazing down on cities below boiling up and swirling around electrons and neutrons when everything was abruptly scattered by a knock on the door and a voice asking when the bathroom might be free given it had already been two-*bloody*-hours? Raising his feet above the bath's end, Leo Szilard slid along his back and let his face sink beneath the water. Only when he resurfaced to a world of white fog did he realise that he had forgotten to take off his spectacles.

6

Wiping his glasses with a wet finger, Leo Szilard decided to pursue his irreconcilable thoughts by walking London's streets. But he had scarcely left his hotel that dreary damp day when, approaching the flank of Russell Square heading towards the British Museum, he was stopped from crossing the road by a red stoplight on Southampton Row.

One light goes out and another lights up, thought Szilard.

And after that?

As he stared at the traffic light's three coloured circles, one illuminated, two dimmed, all other things—traffic, pedestrians, smog, buildings, drizzle—abruptly receded into oblivion.

For several critical seconds nothing else existed in the world—

—and when the world returned it was a world forever changed.

7

One light goes out and another lights up and then another—and another! And another, and another.

These banalities struck Leo Szilard with the force of mystical revelation. But for a moment what that revelation was eluded him. Szilard could see and know but he was unable to say exactly what it was he saw and knew.

What if there were a country where there were many birds? Where every bird shot magically produced two more bullets killing two more birds in turn, and those two dead birds produced four more bullets killing four birds and producing eight bullets? And what if that eight became sixteen and sixteen thirty-two? What then?

Leo Szilard felt a sudden and overwhelming vertigo. The traffic lights swirled all around, multiplying before him as three lights became nine and nine eighty-one. Knowledge collided with imagination to produce a fever of ideas that in turn released more energy into Szilard's suddenly cascading thoughts.

The lights changed.

As he crossed the street he continued staring at the lights. If there were an element which when split by one neutron emitted two neutrons, it would only need massing enough of that element together to sustain more of the same as more atoms were split by more neutrons, creating new, unlimited energy as they continued multiplying.

No one before had ever thought of the idea of a nuclear chain reaction.

8

The idea of a nuclear chain reaction was only the beginning of the revelations Leo Szilard had as the lights changed. If a nuclear chain reaction was possible it would be possible to create atomic energy on an industrial scale. And if atomic energy were possible then an atomic bomb was also possible. But his vision didn't stop there, for it was simultaneously theoretical and political, at once ecstatic and agonising.

A crack opened in his mind and in the universe and immediately began widening. What the owlish young man saw as he found himself falling through it was terrifying. Fiction was transforming into physics and physics into the future in front of the Southampton Row traffic lights, and he saw that future as the abyss that exists before birth and after death, an oblivion at the beginning and end of all human consciousness. If it was possible to build an atomic bomb then it was possible that Hitler could build an atomic bomb and, not only that, given German preeminence in physics, be the first to build it and use it to enslave the world.

Leo Szilard had seen that dismal grey morning what no one else had or for a long time would as the traffic light's red circle ceded to a green—the spectre, huge and terrifying, that would haunt the rest of his life. And at that moment of existential horror he understood what others witnessing the monstrous explosion at Los Alamos twelve years later would only realise too late: that they had become death, destroyers of the world.

9

Within months of his vision in Russell Square Szilard patented the atomic chain reaction. "Knowing what it would mean," he wrote, "and I knew because I had read H. G. Wells—I did not want this patent to become public." He assigned the patent to the British Admiralty so that it might remain secret.

Seeking to quarantine his terrifying revelations, he attempted to persuade eminent colleagues such as Niels Bohr and the Italian physicist Enrico Fermi that atomic weaponry was feasible, and that their nuclear research should therefore be kept secret to ensure Nazi Germany did not get the bomb first. They ignored him. His warnings were seen in equal part as fanciful nonsense while insulting to the notion of an open, international community of scientific scholarship.

Having opened Pandora's box, and aware of the horror that might ensue, Szilard could not help himself. He delved ever deeper inside, pursuing the mystery of the atom while never quite admitting to himself or to others what his research meant and where, inexorably, it was leading. Working hand to mouth through institutions as various as London's St. Bartholomew's Hospital and Cambridge University, something of an intellectual vagabond, almost a philosophical troubadour, taking tribute when offered and accepting patronage when it turned up but refusing to be bound by it, Szilard spent the next five years seeking to prove his theory.

Yet his determination not to alert Nazi scientists doomed his approaches to leading industrialists when pursuing investment in his research. He would tout the commercial applications of nuclear energy as the reward yet refuse to show potential investors the scientific evidence to back up his claims, keeping the necessary information secret. When pressed, he sometimes quoted from *The World Set Free,* saying that Wells's predictions were likely to prove more accurate than those of the scientists who dismissed atomic energy. Businessmen, less than keen to invest in a failed fiction from Edwardian England seemingly no more plausible than a time machine, never ponied up the money Szilard sought.

For five years he worked to find the element that would sustain a nuclear chain reaction. But, focusing on beryllium and then indium, he failed. He was left looking at best a deluded visionary and at worst a scientific shyster. His prospects were far from certain, for, as his friend and fellow physicist Francis Simon wrote to him, "There are quite a few people who are dying to converse with you for a few days but none who would like to offer you a job."

Uninclined to listen to the advice of others while very willing to give it, Szilard was by the winter of 1938 withdrawn, in a depressed state, spending ever more time in the bathtub in his latest room at the King's Crown Hotel in New York, having moved to the United States sensing, with his usual prescience, that the Munich agreement signalled not peace in our time but a Europe hostage to Nazism. Finally, he conceded defeat. He wrote to the British Admiralty asking that his patent no longer be a secret.

Unknown to him, the very same day German scientists led by Otto Hahn in Berlin demonstrated a successful nuclear chain reaction using uranium. It released an unexpected amount of energy, a process they named fission.

10

Leo Szilard learnt the startling news a month later, in January 1939, while visiting his friend, the Hungarian physicist and later Nobel laureate Eugene Wigner, who was ill with jaundice at the Princeton infirmary. Szilard realised his intuition had been right all along and that a chain reaction was possible. Only his choice of element to prove it had been wrong. "All the things H. G. Wells predicted," he later recounted, "appeared suddenly real to me."

His 1933 Russell Square revelation would have been just one more extraordinary insight that had come too early and, because of Szilard's concern to keep it secret, perhaps would have proved to be a dead end were it not that Szilard had in consequence devoted more than half a decade to deeply pondering the technological, military and political consequences of a man-made nuclear chain reaction. And when Wigner told Szilard of the breakthrough with uranium, Szilard, alone in the world, immediately understood the terrifying implications of the discovery.

"You know what fission means?" he told another friend, the physicist Edward Teller. "It means bombs."

Szilard redoubled his urging of his fellow scientists of the need for secrecy. Yet as late as 1939 almost all physicists continued to believe with Rutherford that atomic energy and atomic bombs were moonshine, and that, in any case, science was best served by openness across borders that were now lamentably beginning to close all over Europe.

Szilard's worst fears quickly proved correct. On 29 April 1939 a secret conference in Berlin resulted in the commencement of a Nazi atomic research program, a ban on German uranium exports and the provision for the supply of radium from Czechoslovakian mines to the Third Reich with the aim of developing an atom bomb. Nazi Germany had become the first country in the world to begin actively working to develop nuclear weapons.

11

It was a hot summer's day in early July 1939 when Albert Einstein, who had spent a morning sailing in a small wooden dinghy off Peconic, Long Island, went to answer the door of his holiday home in shorts tied up with string and a pair of size eleven women's sandals that he had bought from the local store in the absence of any men's sandals in his size. To his surprise none other than Leo Szilard and another old colleague from his Berlin days, Eugene Wigner, stood there.

The two men had spent a frustrating, now overly long morning driving from New York to Long Island searching for their former teacher who they had heard was spending his summer holidays there, with no more details other than that he was staying at a cottage owned by a Dr. Moore. Two of the greatest minds in twentieth-century physics had confused place-names and ended up lost on Long Island's south shore instead of its north, taking two hours in the unnecessary detour, then wasting more time while Szilard, a now fat-faced man sounding not unlike Bela Lugosi, took to leaning out the window of Wigner's 1936 Dodge coupe asking Peconic vacationers if they knew where Dr. Moore's cottage might be.

No one knew.

Finally, reasoning every child knew who Einstein was, Szilard decided to ask a young boy with a fishing rod if he knew where the great man was.

He did.

The three men sat on Dr. Moore's porch sipping iced tea and chatting about the latest German atomic discoveries, their own recent experiments and calculations, and how these discoveries might be the basis of atomic bombs. Einstein, who hadn't followed atomic research for some years, was shocked. A pacifist, he nevertheless saw the extraordinary danger of a nuclear-armed Nazi Germany.

It was agreed that Einstein would sign a letter that would be personally delivered by an intermediary to President Roosevelt, alerting him to the danger and seeking support for research into an atomic bomb. The letter was principally Szilard's work, Einstein later saying he "really only acted as a mailbox" for his former student.

The letter pointed out that Nazi Germany was already securing uranium supplies from Czechoslovakia and German research was already repeating American work on uranium. Warning of "extremely powerful bombs of a new type," just one of which "carried by a boat and exploded in a port, might very well destroy the whole port together with some of the surrounding territory," the letter urged the government to take "quick action."

Roosevelt was persuaded. In October 1939 the US government began work to develop an atom bomb, leading to the later historic Manhattan Project.

12

Szilard remained an influential and at times pivotal force in the bomb's development through the war. Though his energies were devoted to defeating the Nazis and ensuring that they were not the first with the bomb, his efforts were perversely limited by official persecution. His independence of mind and approach enraged General Leslie Groves, a portly bull of a man put in charge of the Manhattan Project and described by a fellow officer as "the biggest sonovabitch I've ever met in my life, but also one of the most capable."

Groves loathed Leo Szilard. "I am not prejudiced," Groves said in his defence. "I don't like certain Jews and I don't like certain well-known characteristics of theirs, but I am not prejudiced." He observed that were the United States "a country like Germany" there were a dozen scientists "we should have shot right off. And another dozen we could have shot for suspicion or carelessness." If Groves had been allowed an execution list Leo Szilard almost certainly would have been at its top. He unsuccessfully sought to have Szilard interned for the war's duration and had the FBI follow and investigate Szilard.

The agents for their part described a man "inclined to be rather absent-minded and eccentric . . . [He will] go out on the street without his coat or hat and frequently looks up and down the street as if he were watching for someone or did not know for sure where he wanted to go."

At times there would be upwards of six agents watching Szilard breakfast in a diner. Szilard compared Groves's methods to the Nazis', but he met the torment with good humour, offering the hapless shadows coffees, inviting them into his cab, even proffering umbrellas when it was raining.

Despite Groves's persecution, Szilard continued with his work. A critical step in developing an atom bomb was building a nuclear reactor. To succeed, a substance—known as a moderator—was needed to slow down the speed of neutrons so that they would strike enough nearby uranium atoms to create a nuclear chain reaction. Szilard discovered—typically not in the lab but over lunch in conversation with some contractors—that commercial grade graphite contained boron. Szilard knew boron absorbed neutrons, thus preventing a chain reaction.

On 2 December 1942, in a squash court beneath the stands of the University of Chicago's Stagg Field football stadium, the world's first man-made nuclear reaction took place in a nuclear reactor built by Szilard and Fermi, now a Nobel laureate, using, thanks to Szilard's insight, a newly developed, highly purified graphite.

"There was a crowd there and when it dispersed, Fermi and I stayed there alone," Szilard later wrote. "I shook hands with Fermi and I said that I thought this day would go down as a black day in the history of mankind. I was quite aware of the dangers. Not because I am so wise but because I have read a book written by H. G. Wells called *The World Set Free*."

13

Szilard's indefatigable advocacy of self-censorship on atomic research was also finally yielding results. Scientists were breaking with long-standing tradition and no longer publicly publishing papers on the subject, thereby starving Nazi scientists of knowledge of critical breakthroughs that would have greatly helped them build an atomic bomb.

Lacking that knowledge and lacking a Szilard, unaware of the problem of boron contamination, the German scientists had wrongly concluded in January 1940 that graphite would not work as a moderator. The Germans turned to the use of heavy water in its place, a far rarer substance that required extensive electrolysis to isolate it from normal water. The principal source of heavy water in Europe was a Norwegian hydroelectricity plant at Vemork which the Allies were able to successfully cripple through partisan sabotage and aerial bombing. In consequence, the Germans never succeeded in building a successful nuclear reactor. Even before Germany's unconditional surrender in May 1945 it was clear that the Nazis had no nuclear weaponry. The target for the bomb was now to be Japan which the United States knew had no capacity to build an atomic bomb.

The rationale for Szilard's support for the bomb vanished. Einstein later said he would never have signed his famous letter to Roosevelt if he had known the Germans didn't have the bomb. Faced with the imminent birth of the nuclear era for which he bore so much responsibility, a far-fetched fiction he had helped transform into fact, Szilard feared a new era of barbarism loomed unless immediate steps were taken.

14

In the latter part of *The World Set Free* the world is saved during a global nuclear war by the unlikely figure of Leblanc, the French ambassador to the United States, who convenes "a last desperate conference to 'save humanity.'" Leblanc, small, bald, bespectacled, "with his transparent childish innocence . . . possessed of one clear persuasion, that war must end" appeals directly to the president "for the Americans were also among the simple peoples by whom the world was saved."

The paradox of Leo Szilard is that as his life progresses, this brilliant man with an almost mystical ability to see the future nevertheless seems to come under the spell of a mediocre novel so completely that at first the book appears to predict his life only to then mock it.

And so, as if aping Leblanc, Szilard secured a meeting with Eleanor Roosevelt, the president's influential wife, scheduled for 8 May 1945, to press the need for delaying any use of the atomic bomb and developing a system of international controls. His hopes for the meeting died with Roosevelt on 12 April.

Szilard's torment was only beginning. In late May, weeks before the first atomic bomb was tested in New Mexico on 16 July, he passed a memorandum to James Byrnes, soon to be secretary of state for the new president, Harry Truman, for him to deliver to Truman. Szilard asked that the president withhold his approval of using the bomb against Japan, pleading that Japan be given advance warning, arguing for a demonstration bomb explosion to be witnessed by Japanese officials to show the terrifying power the United States could now unleash.

Byrnes never delivered the memorandum.

The day after the first atomic bomb test Szilard, frightened by what he had been central in creating, forwarded a petition to Truman signed by 155 Manhattan Project scientists that advanced a moral argument against the bomb's use against Japan, warning that any subsequent global nuclear confrontation could be catastrophic. There would have been more signatories but J. Robert Oppenheimer, director at Los Alamos, forbade the petition's circulation there.

General Groves delayed the petition's delivery. To negate its impact he ordered a poll of his scientists only to discover that 83 percent supported a demonstration of the bomb to Japanese officials before using it. He buried these findings also.

When Szilard tried to publish the petition the following month, Groves had it classified. It was not declassified until 1961. There is no evidence Truman ever read it. On 25 July 1945 he authorised the dropping of an atomic bomb on Japan as soon as weather permitted after 3 August. There were four possible sites. One was Hiroshima.

15

Captain Paul Tibbets was given twelve cyanide capsules before departing the Tinian Island base for Hiroshima. If the *Enola Gay* was shot down, each crew member was to swallow one so that they could not be taken captive and reveal any information. Tibbets was ordered to shoot anyone who refused. Mid-flight he told his co-pilot, Robert Lewis. Lewis responded by showing him a pack of condoms he carried in his pocket ready for the postwar party.

"Bomb away!" said Thomas Ferebee, as the great silver-plated B-29 banked up and away and 60,000 or 80,000 or 140,000 Japanese souls passed through the plane's silver aluminium cladding and superstructure and the aircrew's leather air suits, penetrating their skin and bones and organs such that they lit up as if they had swallowed a light more brilliant than the sun. This worried Thomas Ferebee. Over the plane's intercom he asked Captain Paul Tibbets if he would still be able to have children.

16

In Los Alamos that evening, Oppenheimer, the head of the project there, took to the stage in front of an assembly of all those who had worked on the bomb. "I'll never forget his walk," the physicist Isidor Rabi later recalled. "His walk was like *High Noon* . . . this kind of strut. He had done it." Oppenheimer raised both hands and clasped them together "like a prize-winning boxer."

The crowd cheered.

"Using atomic bombs against Japan is one of the greatest blunders of history," Szilard wrote the following day to his close friend, later to be his wife, Gertrud Weiss. "I went out of my way (and very much so) in order to prevent it but as today's papers show, without success."

"It was one of the most important letters he ever wrote to me," Weiss later said, adding, "I always thought it was his way of apologising."

17

Thomas Ferebee died in 2000, survived by his four sons and five grandchildren. Time can never be stopped or reversed, and nor can the unimaginable suffering and immeasurable death be stopped or reversed. To suggest otherwise is a form of kitsch. To suggest otherwise would be to pretend that we know what happened at Hiroshima. But no one knows what happened at

Hiroshima. Everyone who knew had already passed through Thomas Ferebee's body as pure energy, lighting his body up like a neon tube.

What if vengeance and atonement both are simply the lie that time can be reversed and thereby some equality, some equilibrium restored, some justice had? Is it simply truer to say Hiroshima happened, Hiroshima is still happening, and Hiroshima will always happen?

18

Three Japanese women came to see my father many years later. They came with gifts. They asked him to tell his story and they listened. They said they were sorry.

There was a sense of strange ceremony, the awkwardness of ensuring something exquisitely fragile was not dropped before being given and received. There was a reserve on the part of both my father and the women, perhaps explicable as a nervousness about giving offence where none was intended.

They were part of a group of Japanese women committed to exposing Japanese war crimes. Two were middle-aged and one was elderly. They were brave and they were dignified. The eldest was their leader. She had survived the Tokyo fire bombing. My father expressed his sorrow.

His children and his grandchildren were all there. We watched this meeting with its strange weight of human dignity and goodness. I could not ever have believed that saying sorry might mean so much. None was their government. None bore responsibility. No one spoke for anyone other than themselves. Nothing said or done had any national consequence. Yet in that strange communion lay liberation. What other answer can any of us make to the terrible question of history?

19

Thomas Ferebee's body *was* lit up like a neon tube, his body *is* lighting up like a neon tube, his body *will* always light up like a neon tube as until the end of all things the suffering of the dead illuminates the living.

That's life.

Six

1

I must be two years old when we stand in the departing mist on some embankment or rise looking down at the flooded South Esk flowing around our village of Longford in which we are now cut off, my mother's warm hand enclosing mine. A vast flatness of water moving imperceptibly and inexorably, which is to say strangely and outwardly not at all, erasing detail, labour, the frail markings of man. Before us, everything is transforming into a mystery of water as inscrutable as a floating mirror.

I didn't know it was a river. I thought it was the world, that the world moved. I thought my mother meant me to understand that it would be necessary to ride it and move with it somehow if we were to live. If she had said we must row our home to another world, I would have asked if I might help pull an oar.

From the beginning I was haunted by rivers.

I remember above all my mother's excitement—of life upended, perhaps thrilling to the loss of control, or adventure, or the whole world turned fluid and upside down; the possibility of finding freedom in the world beyond human beings when it is denied to you otherwise. For one glorious moment any loss seemed worth the cost.

2

After some time there appears out of the mist a car, a Ford Zephyr overloaded with children and suitcases and bags, driving along a new road in 1963, a muddy track slashing a seemingly negligible gash through a temperate rainforest. In this world where the measure of all things is not man-made, it seems at first the merest scratch, a slight wound that will quickly heal over, rather than what it is, the beginning of something gangrenous and fatal.

Here we all are in the Ford Zephyr, sprawled out and jammed up on the parcel shelf, out the window screaming into the rain and rainforest and spread-eagled over the transmission hump, one brother wearing a snorkel to avoid another brother's farts, pushing and shoving and being shoved until parting when our father's frustrated hand flails over the front bench seat into the back to re-establish order, his disembodied voice crying out in exasperation, "I don't care who started it! I'll finish it!" before a wild swerve throws us all back on top of each other and the squealing and shoving start all over again.

For a little longer steam will still drift from the forest floor in the sunlight that pierces the Gondwanan caravanserai enveloping that lonely crowded car making its way to our new home in Rosebery, a raw mining village in Tasmania's still remote west: celery top pines, pandani, Tasmanian laurels and peppers and leather-woods, the giant manferns and primeval sassafras and craggy myrtles, the rainforest that no one then knows is the second largest of its kind in the world with its plants and trees as old as the dinosaurs.

If we were to rise above it, above the mountains, and the island at the end of the world in which they sit, would we be able to see advancing from another direction *Western time*—with its insatiable greed and its monstrous appetite, *Western time* with its new machines, *Western time* that will shortly dam the rivers and gobble the rainforest—would we see all that, and with it the coming reign of those promoting infinite theft from a finite world?

No, for that world and its wonders still seem endless.

3

But even then the rainforest was being corroded. Soon it will be pocked with the scattered melanomas of cattle runs, pine and eucalypt plantations, fire-scabbed here and there, to say nothing of a general, growing inanity, roads to nowhere, tourist resorts, unworked mines and crowded geo-tagged Insta sites. These though will be but small insults compared to what is coming.

Over the following decades the rain will lessen, at first imperceptibly and then dramatically, and what remains of the rainforest will slowly start drying out and dying off. For a moment or two more though the myrtles, cicatrices weeping fern and fungi, will tower and teeter, old thespians taking a final bow made more compelling by a dramatic backdrop of still steeply wooded gullies and ridges.

Then they will start to burn.

The intricate, myriad, miraculous relationships the sum of which is Tasmanian rainforest, a precise confusion of tree, fern, moss, fungi and microbe, of animal and bird and insect, fish and invertebrate, that might be better described as an unknown civilisation, will, along with these words, become no more than the lost jetsam of time.

A silent revolution will sweep it all away, its Robespierres and Lenins and Khomeinis a conga line of faceless CEOs, investors, economists and politicians, destroying everything in which a soul—or my own at least—could once find purpose and resonance. For a great crime there should be a great criminal, not so many so small, so immemorable.

In any case, what remains will be a wet gravel desert amidst which will be found impoundments of dead water, ash heaps and tailings dams, charred tree stumps and open-cut holes, rusting derricks and cranes and ancillary structures, bricks and corro where women once washed in the incessant rain and the cold, so much detritus mirrored in dark, toxic puddles oozing heavy metals and acid and poisons. But of that annihilated civilisation: nothing.

A masked owl, the last of its kind, its riddling face outlined with a heart and bisected by a murderer's beak, will spread its ermine spotted wings and leave the last tree, searching for a home now gone forever, chittering an imminent oblivion.

We will have arrived back on Wells's time traveller's dying beach, alone, in a dimming twilight. If I were a sculptor this would be my art: rusting machinery without purpose rising out of oily scum. People might see it as beauty or meaning. But they would be wrong. It would be what remains.

Nothing.

4

Far below the small lounge room of the little government timber bungalow into which we moved in Rosebery, replete with the miracle of an indoor toilet, perched on the edge of a deep rainforested valley, I was taken with the sight far below of a serpentine line curving in and out of mist-puffs through that endless green world. This new river captivated me. Whenever it first entered my consciousness—four? five?—I already knew the rainforest that lay between me and the river was too thick for a small child to find a way through. And I would again turn away from the window and back to the black-and-white television with its very small bulbous blue-hued screen set in a deep wooden cabinet.

I would seek to make out what was happening through the lines of static that fell across the blurry images of *The Cisco Kid,* a cowboy show from the early fifties that formed part of the few hours of television on the single government station that were transmitted across the emptied wildlands and the silenced button-grass plains to our remote mining town. In bad weather—and the weather was mostly bad—we saw only squalls of static invading the screen as a hailstorm of dots. Cisco and his sidekick Pancho occasionally blurrily ventured out of the tempest inside the cathode ray tube only to be washed away by synoptic waves before vanishing altogether while my little sister and I took turns to stand up, holding the antenna, a horizontal wire spiral, this way or that in a battle, forever forlorn, to have them return.

As the television's squall continued, we would invent our own scenarios and add in other characters—ourselves, or someone like Chad Morgan whose remarkable buck-toothed visage we sometimes glimpsed between static storms on *Reg Lindsay's Country Hour,* which we similarly attempted watching with our father on a late Saturday afternoon and during which our distant father would occasionally dance with us. He would pick us up and we would slowly waltz, my father dancing to a different time. I don't recall him ever holding me other than those few dances.

Rosebery was the wettest town in Australia in 1964 or 1965, wetter even than tropical Tully, traditional holder of the Australian record with its monsoonal rains breaking hard on the Atherton Tablelands. It was a world of water. When it wasn't rain it was fog and when it wasn't fog it was rain. We lived within rain's tempestuous world, accepting of it, if sometimes astonished, occasionally annoyed, and every now and then marvelling for there was no end to it. I could check which year was the wettest, or whether either is even correct, but this is an account of memory, not fact, and facts are not how we know ourselves, while memory—its tricks, its evasions, its silences, its inventions, its inevitable questions—is who we become as we shuffle around in a circle in that small lounge room while the incessant rain continues crashing on our uninsulated tin roof and brushes our windows, the TV again irrelevant, my father lost in another dance and other, older memories as we slowly circle his past together.

5

Sometimes one of my father's cobbers would drop by. Joe D—, another POW and champion boxer who ran the Williamsford pub and who in 1939 famously beat the celebrated Victorian Archie Kemp, a Chinese-Australian from Tasmania who later died in the ring. Archie's brother would marry my aunt Muriel and then abandon her and their children, leaving Muriel to raise her family in appalling poverty in Fitzroy. In the end her children were taken away from her.

Then there was Bunny D—, an Aboriginal piner who had been in the camps with Dad and who was famed for his bush skills. Bunny liked a fight. Once he took Dad to one of the miners' pubs for a drink only to do all he could to incite a fight, saying to my father, as he sought to restrain Bunny and keep the peace, "If she's on, I know you'll back me." When no one would bother with an old drunk, Bunny looked ruefully at my father and said, "You don't get rats out of mice."

Another time Bunny turned up at our house worse for wear. "He's a good little bloke," he said of one of my brothers, and gave him a pound note. Rather pleased, my brother went out to the kitchen and when he returned Bunny said, "Here's another good little bloke," and gave my brother another pound note. My brother, sensing a pattern, returned a third time, and was rewarded with our mother cuffing him, making him empty his pockets and give Mr. D— back his money.

Bunny lived with a woman in a solitary hut at Parrawe. There was nothing else at Parrawe that I remember. The hut was by the side of the road backing onto a button-grass plain that to me as a child seemed to run away into infinity. In a way it did, one of a series of grassland corridors through the rainforest created over millennia by Aboriginal burning. For all that, it was a lonely place that seemed the beginning of some portal, something down which I didn't yet wish to travel, and which I suppose I now am.

6

In 1966, head on my mother's lap and her hand on my head, I was lying across the front bench seat of the family car, now an EH Holden wagon. For once, my father was driving. It was night, I was five, in pain from another ear infection that was pushing me deeper into an inner world, and we were driving the winding muddy track, the one road out of Rosebery through the Tarkine's primeval forests, headed towards Turners Beach on the northwest coast, and the other great pole of our lives, our shack, a vertical board hut with a fire and tank with a single tap and little else, the only home my parents owned until they moved to the island's capital when I was nine.

I watched as great myrtles and giant manferns momentarily loomed over us, as if we were passing through an avenue of some ancient world throwing noirish shadows before sliding back into blackness as we drove on. Stumbling on Angkor Wat's ruins would not have made any greater an impression on my child's mind as we slowly made our circuitous way down that track into Hellyer Gorge.

I woke pitching forward as the car abruptly slew to a halt. Within moments my parents were outside searching in the weak glow of the car's headlights on that lonely road for the Tasmanian tiger—even then a mythical creature—which had just crossed in front of our car. I followed, confused, feeling the wetness of fog beading on my face, seeing only puddles in the dimly lit muddy gravel.

Following on from another Tasmanian government-sponsored program of extermination, the last-known tiger—a remarkable wolf-like marsupial with the striping of a tiger, the male with a two-headed penis and the female with a pouch in which she carried her pups—had died in a Hobart zoo in 1936. Sightings such as my parents' in remote wildlands continued for a few decades but it was already by the 1960s a mythical creature. *Thylacinus cynocephalus* was declared officially extinct in 1982. So much of the world from my childhood has gone with it. I was born into the autumn of things.

7

One of my strongest and most enduring memories of that time is of something that might never have happened:

it is me as a very young child in Williamsford, still then a small mining town a few miles south of Rosebery, near Montezuma Falls, with a mighty haulage way that always astonished me as a child with its vertiginous wonder. We are visiting someone my mother knew and we are taking biscuits still warm from the oven to have with the tea. We make our way along wet, greasy planks that trace a rude path through the mud that slops behind a street of wooden and tin cottages, dilapidated and makeshift. Women are hard at work out the back under rudimentary lean-tos to shelter them from the incessant rain, in the mud and squalor, boiling clothes, stirring wood-fired boilers with long paddle sticks, worn grey and feathery from time and wash water. From the rear the cottages are little more than shanties cheek by jowl. The poverty of the sight shocked me even as a child.

Now I wonder if I ever saw it at all.

For the memory seems much more of the 1930s than the 1960s. Was it some newsreel or some conflation, some trick of memory? The women, the kids around them, appear to me now as ghosts and one woman's dark eyes stare at me. I don't know why she singled me out to remember her so many years later. I remember her so vividly yet I cannot even say if she ever truly existed. The town she lived in is gone, not a house left, and all that remains is one more spectral west coast Tasmanian landscape of broken bricks, moss-mottled, crumbling concrete footings, rusting corro fragments, and occasional inexplicable gravel hillocks overrun with rainforest and heath.

The more I look at her the more she resembles my father's mother who died long before I was born: scrawny, consumptive, worn out, hollow-cheeked, exhausted by life. The memory is bathed in an aura which only makes me more suspicious but I remember the warmth of the home-cooked biscuits I wanted to eat, the boards through the mud over which we threaded our way, my mother pulling on my hand to draw me away, to stop me staring.

And yet, thinking on it, I am no longer sure if these are true memories or tricks of my mind as the mud shapeshifts into something it is not, a track from which my mother and I gaze up through the rainforest at Montezuma waterfall—was that the same day or another? Yet with my already poor eyesight what grips me is not the fall's violent grandeur but the intimate green world at its base, moss gardens of tiny peach-tipped myrtles and luminous fungi growing out of fallen tree barrels. Whole and seemingly solid yet rotted completely, the tree barrels collapse into peat the moment I touch them, the way my memories crumble into questions now.

8

Once, other people lived here, moving in and out as millennia passed and Ice Ages came and went and the rainforest and heaths followed, swapping places as the Earth warmed and cooled and warmed and finally began to overheat. They marked the land in many ways, some still evident in the corridors of button grass, their petroglyphs of circles within circles and the profoundly moving remains of their villages, their massive middens of seashells now washing away as seas rise, the clusters of large circular cups out of which their beehive homes once arose. If this book were the forty thousand years they have existed on this island, Europeans would enter the story only in the last page and a half.

But then came the invasion. It was, as an 1830s Van Diemonian attorney-general wrote, "A war of extermination," a war the Tasmanian Aboriginal people finally lost.

There remains to this day debate as to whether this war was a genocide. Raphael Lemkin, the remarkable Jewish lawyer who in the wake of the Second World War coined the word, the concept, and the legal definition of genocide, was under no illusion. After a lifetime of study and reflection, Lemkin concluded that the crime of genocide was one with deep historical roots. Amidst the chapters of his unpublished history of genocide was one devoted to the fate of the Tasmanian Aboriginal people.

Exiled to slums and an island reserve and silence, renamed and reviled as islanders and abos and boongs and half-castes and troublemakers, they could be called any vile humiliation imaginable but what they were: the original human inhabitants of the island. Whenever they stood up and gave tongue to that truth, they discovered it was an obscenity, the most insulting lie, and they were told that most Tasmanian of jokes: that the last of their kind had died out a century before. That they didn't exist.

9

Of a night our mother read to me and my little sister. Books had an odd place in our home, both revered and absent. We had perhaps a shelf of them on a bookcase as small and plain as a kitchen cupboard. My father's mother and father—my grandparents—were, as I earlier mentioned, illiterate. My father had, I suspect in consequence, a sense of the magic of words that never left him, an awareness that those twenty-six abstract symbols could liberate if you understood them and oppress if you didn't. He told me the written word was the first beautiful thing he ever knew, a line I stole and used elsewhere. What is a writer but a robber and what is the history of literature but a milky way of theft? He would often recite poetry from memory—the nineteenth-century English poets, Shakespeare, the early twentieth-century Australians, Lawson, C. J. Dennis, and the bard of the Australian-Irish peasantry, John O'Brien. He would pause to repeat a turn of words, a phrase, marvelling at it, and then he and my mother would parse the phrase, the meaning of a word choice.

My favourites were two river books, *The Wind in the Willows* and a picture book called *Peter the Pirate* that Mate had given me for a birthday. Each night's bedtime reading by our mother would be followed by our evening prayers, which always invoked the same formula: God bless—followed by a roll call of family that swelled and shrank according to my mother's patience.

My five brothers and sisters, my mother and father and Mate were many nights more than enough to list but sometimes the idea of family would enlarge as my sister and I competed to include those of the fifty-one first cousins we could remember along with uncles and aunts and great-aunts and great-uncles and then the ever more distant and unreliably related. After all, we lived in a clannish way with at one time an aunt taking ill and her seven children coming to live with us until she was better, and all thirteen kids then going down with chickenpox.

It intrigued us to see at what point our mother might break, our first taste of how overt piety begins in perversity. Inevitably, such calling for marathon divine blessing would collapse under the weight of numbers, the way in which lists always exclude, and who was listed only reminding you of the unlisted and raising ethical questions that remain beyond me to this day: why her and not him and him and not her? If not all why bother with any? These questions that no one really worries about other than philosophers and wedding planners are, I suppose, fundamental, for they pose riddles about who we love and why we love, none of which worried our mother when she told us she wasn't playing this game any longer.

As a child all these thoughts would sometimes leave me dizzy, until my mother with her soft voice, that northwest Tasmanian brogue rich with its slight smoothed-off gravel, would tell us our family was enough for tonight, that God looked after the rest, her rough working hands and large fingers sweeping the fine blond hair on my forehead into a part, her touch and smell of soap reassuring, and after she left I would lie there, enwombed in the rain that fell with a tremendous cacophony on the tin roof, the incessant rain that fell night after night, week after week, month after month, and watch the occasional car headlights throw long rippling shadows across the far wall.

I worried at being suddenly alone with my mother gone, the light out. After a further time I fell into one of those black ripples and found myself riding along its current in a little boat, replete with sail and friends, and me, free of family, leaving my world, dreaming of a sunny riverbank where Ratty and Mole boated and Peter the Pirate played, and I continued on my way down the river having adventures. Here and there a jetty beckoned and a path led up to Uncle B—'s failing farm with its barn full of the sweet, intoxicating smell of dried hay and my wonderful older girl cousins, and I felt my gathering shyness, my growing inability to understand what was being said and to say words properly and be understood, and so I continued heading down the river towards my destiny as the mine's siren sounded, as the earth thumped with some underground explosion, and the rain slapped the tin roof.

10

It was in Rosebery that I decided at the age of four—absurdly, pointlessly, and for what reason I have to this day no idea, given that I couldn't then write a word—that I wished to be a writer. My first efforts were little books I wrote for my big sister who had gone to teachers' college in distant Launceston—a small provincial town which in my childhood evoked the metropolitan astonishment of Manhattan. I would write them on pink pad paper and my mother—acting on my wishes—would staple the pages together, bind them with black electrical tape and post them to my sister. Though they had sentences and paragraphs and pictures, the only vaguely comprehensible part were the pictures, for I was unable to write more than a handful of letters, and the sentences were illustrations of sentences and paragraphs—the idea and the architecture of a book, in other words, if not the exact meaning.

On the back my mother would write out the story, my first translations, I suppose. But none of this was the point of the books: I missed my big sister greatly and the point of the books was to smuggle a message of love to her, and each book, every faux sentence and every scrawled picture of a word was simply saying that one word over and over. And so at the beginning I learnt this: the words of a book are never the book, the soul of it is everything.

11

Many years later, when I went to Oxford, I studied history, an idea of time formed over 3,000 years of human experience in Europe, which, I discovered, made perfect sense of European time, stopping at all stations of European progress and European thought. It was a straight railway line that perfectly mirrored an experience that became an idea, and an idea that became experience, and an experience that became European thought and then the European novel.

But it made no sense of Tasmania.

In Tasmania, history did not hold and reality was otherwise: history constantly failed, history constantly recurred not as answers or comfort, not as a story of progress, but as a massacre site, a napalmed logging clearfell, convict words that spoke of what couldn't be spoken, mythical beings long dead that kept returning, haunting, asking of me something I have spent a life trying and failing to answer. I was the issue of a genocide and a slave society, and nothing ever quite went forward and everything finally returned, as I was to also. There was no straight line of history. There was only a circle. Everything, finally, was as the ancient petroglyphs depicted it: a circle circling within circles, the island's great idea of time formulated over 40,000 years of human experience.

12

When I first attempted writing novels as an adult I wrote tales of cities and crowds, the great tropes of European modernism. Every word was rubbish. I'd never seen a city or known a crowd. My first experience of a crowd was in London at the age of twenty-four. I was frightened. It was inconceivable that there could be so many people and not one person knew you nor you them. And there amidst innumerable millions of fellow human beings I felt the most terrible solitude that was also an inconsolable fear. There was no anchor, there were no roots, there was no river down which I might return. All I knew was what I first experienced as a child, unsayable and unwritten, a world within which the measure of things was not man-made and of which you existed as a minuscule fragment. Finding words for it was, in one sense, my life's work and my life's failure.

Now that world we oddly disdain as the nonhuman—as though we are somehow separate of it—is vanishing. And with it, unnoticed, a different, larger way of being human than that propounded by Western art and thought. Could it be what is being lost with that world is us?

At some point I came to understand that I wrote from the front lines of a war about which most have no idea. For a long time I could not understand that it was possible to be both on the side that has the power, that has unleashed the destruction, vast as it is indescribable, and, at the same time, be on the side that loses everything.

To do that you have to return to a child blinking in the rain, staring into the darkness, looking for something that his parents saw only an instant before and which has already vanished for all time, never to return.

That's life.

Seven

1

Given television in Rosebery had largely amounted to serial acts of individual creation by me and my little sister it was ironic that many years later I found myself returning there with a BBC documentary crew. We landed in a seaplane on what remains of the river: one of three flooded impoundments. We were picked up in his old ute by the town publican, moonlighting from his work. Driving down the mountain pass into the town, the show's urbane English host leant across the dog-haired backseat of the battered Toyota Hilux. Placing a fraternal arm over the Peli cases of camera gear he asked if I'd seen the new Stoppard yet.

When *Rosencrantz and Guildenstern* had first charmed audiences in London in 1967, I was wandering the main street of Rosebery, forever crowded in my mind, taking in with a child's wonder the fistfights, the strong odours of tobacco smoke and the fecund yeast of stale beer, sometimes venturing into pubs and bookies and being greeted affably and kindly in a forest of damp trousers and accents of Europe's postwar diaspora, those I was chastised by my mother for calling reffos or wogs, I can't recall which word, one of the words everyone then used, and she saying that when they came to church, as many of the Poles and Germans and Italians and Czechs and Yugsolavs did, they were all equal before God and we were no more than they. And perhaps among their number was someone who had witnessed his Czech family being rounded up and sent off to Nazi death camps. Or, equally plausible, someone who had helped round up or murder them.

I felt an embarrassment bringing the BBC crew to Rosebery as the subject of their film was me, but more than me, an idea of *literature* of which I was to become part. Whatever Rosebery was, Rosebery was not *literature*. Rosebery and Tasmania with it were a world which had never really existed in novels. And denied the liberating lies of the novel, Tasmania tended to novelise its own experience. The island divined itself not through the prisms of ideology, religion, aesthetics, or politics as elsewhere, but through stories, endless and endlessly digressive, open to all to add and subtract, multiply and divert and reinvent. Sport was the only art allowed and its events and stars were most loved when they inclined to the operatic. Small jokes became freighted with larger meaning: when the governor was coming to Rosebery, some miners stole the official limousine with its vice-regal regalia and drove it around the town with an Aboriginal man known as Blacktracker sitting in the governor's seat, waving to the locals, a bitter joke which cut every way and was all the more tragic for being comic for both black and white, and all the more comic for being bitter to all. Such was our theatre.

How could I say to the charming English television host that there was an antiquity to this place, a sense of deep time if you just stopped and waited, which was inescapable and perhaps unreachable in *literature,* perhaps even unsayable as *literature*? That the feeling standing next to a 13,000-year-old Huon pine on Mount Read made all of European literature look like the wild posturings of adolescents: so much juvenilia. There was no Stoppard to be had in Rosebery, no literary allusions. There was nothing charmed in that broken, breaking world. And yet human beings had lived here for twice as long as they had in Europe, and amidst the latter survivors of one apocalypse there also dwelled the survivors of an earlier holocaust.

No, I replied to the host, I hadn't seen the new Stoppard.

Mixed reviews, the host replied.

2

As we drove into the battered town, I could still see the people who once lived there—the carnival that was the main street of Rosebery, a marvellous mouth full of broken teeth and rancid odours, the pubs with their drunks and excitement and fraternity, the fug of fags and wet logs smouldering, the way so many homes smelt then, the welcoming damp astringency of burning eucalypt and myrtle, with an undertone of the ammoniacal closeness of laundry hanging from wooden racks roped up to the kitchen ceiling to dry.

I am at a friend's birthday party as a seven-year-old, all we kids happily feeding on fairy bread sandwiches and cakes, the first time I had seen the little pink lamington butterfly cakes with cream sandwiched beneath a flap that rose like an open dormer window, fringed with a tassel-edged frippery of desiccated coconut. The adults are a little giggly and loud and relaxed with beer and sherry. My school friend's father, a miner who played in the miners' marching band, sits slumped in an old armchair. The armchair has large arms covered in a fraying fabric though of what colour I can't recall. In one hand he holds a small six-ounce glass of the type in which beer was drunk in those days on the island, while with the fingers of his other hand he absentmindedly plays with the coconut fibre jutting out of the ripped arm of his armchair, twirling the stiff curling threads first this way and then that.

I watch him, he is looking a little bleary, perhaps exhausted from his work, or perhaps something else, he clearly has had a few drinks, and a woman—his wife?—brings him a black case from which he takes a piece of elaborate, ornate brass tubing. Before picking up the trumpet he wipes it a few times with a piece of old rag, then begins tap-tapping out tunes. He stops and smiles, his exhaustion giving way to a lazy, ecstatic energy. A life spent listening to music since has been for me no more than an endlessly recurring attempt to recapture those moments in which a drunk miner enchanted me with his trumpet playing, some clear, joyful wonder that pierced and uplifted the wounded world around it.

The music ends, it is morning and the whole main street of Rosebery is as I have never seen it: crowded and yet silent. Moving through the crowd is a long column of people following a car. My mother and I watch. She is holding my hand firmly as I have a tendency to wander away. When I ask my mother what is happening, she tells me it is the funeral of a miner who was killed at work. And I cannot understand how a man would be allowed to be killed doing his job. Through the people on the street I feel the grief flowing, the immense gravity of living in the wake of death.

That's life.

3

When I grew up it took me some time to understand what people meant when they talked about women's hands being beautiful when the hands about which they talked seemed unformed, so slight and unmarked as to appear as if they had never lived. My mother's hands were not like that. They revelled in life. If her tongue was vivid her hands were eloquent.

Large-fingered and strong, bearing cuts and scrapes from housework, the crescent of her nail cuticles frequently white-rimed with flour, these hands plied me with affection and food throughout my childhood. They lived and were lively, volatile and emotional.

Sometimes when we were on her beloved north-west coast driving along the new highway—and it was she who mostly drove, not my father—which was then being cut through the region's rich chocolate red basalt soils, she would bemoan the sadness of such beautiful earth being buried beneath a road. At the large cuttings she would abruptly stop—she always drove the family car with a certain gusto, and spoke admiringly of Gelignite Jack, a rally car driver of the 1950s famed for throwing sticks of gelignite out of his car while he raced to deter competitors—and have us fill discarded superphosphate bags she had got from one of her brothers with the red soil.

I still seem to be holding that plastic bag as my mother shovels the heavy red soil on the highway's verge, watching horrified as cars fly by and in my shame turning my stare to the dirt, fat and full as some lardy dough, as it slowly peels off the shovel's spoon, sensuous and so full of life, while she, excited, is not there with me or us, but somewhere else in time and space, standing on the sled her father's beloved Clydesdale, Prince, drags across the paddock with lunch for her father, until she and I both begin dissolving into the lengthening shadow thrown by the road cutting's embankment in the late sun, both of us growing vaporous in our fallible labour of memory.

When we made it home to Hobart in the island's south where the soil was miserable grey clay, she would empty the bags over a patch of the backyard that was henceforth decreed the potato patch, her hands picking up the greasy lumps and crumbling them.

"Soil!" she would cry triumphantly—and it was as if it were not her talking to me but her beloved long-dead farmer father talking to her, the one he had always called his little tomboy.

And as I looked up, the fecund red earth crumbs trickled through those rough fingers.

"Now *that's* soil, son."

4

She was impetuous, adventurous, boisterous, funny. And all these things were beaten out of her by Mate and the convent school to which she was sent. But they were never destroyed. "Oh, she was cruel," my uncle Pat said of Mate, and then told me of how he, the eldest, had been what he termed "a love child," and Mate never forgave him the shame and guilt she carried in consequence, beating him and the next born, my mother, with great violence.

My mother needed adventures and vistas, movement and variety. She should have raced Formula 1 or built a vehicle to tackle the land speed record. But in the mid-twentieth century she had to make do with stillness, a suburban backlot, an EH Holden and six kids. She was Lawrentian in her fervour and *life force,* but there was nothing tragic about her. There was too much life in her for that, too much largeness for it to be contained or crippled, and somehow, in a vast achievement that only now do I begin to appreciate, she never gave in to the narrow-minded resentments that are sometimes visited on children by frustrated parents.

Once—but once only—I saw another side. In her seventies she came to visit me—no doubt she brought some food, she never arrived *empty-handed,* and when she was leaving we somehow—I don't remember how—ended up sitting in her car and she spoke of how difficult our father was, how since his retirement he would sort out her cupboards and drawers expressing dissatisfaction with the way she kept them. Her cupboards and her drawers, her smallest of dominions and one of the few allowed her. And she began to cry, there on the street, sitting in her car, my tough old mum, crying, her large hands all the time grasping the steering wheel, as though there was still some turning down the road that she might yet take, just as her father's hands had once grasped the plough handles as Prince took the weight, the leather harness tautened, and the plough began to run, with her, a child, following behind in the furrow, watching the rich red volcanic dirt turning outwards with its perpetually welcoming hands.

5

In my memory her hands are always wrinkled. Perhaps as a fair-skinned woman she had wrinkled early and I was in any case born late in the family lineage, the fifth of six children. She was forty-two, and I never saw her naturally auburn hair that Mate used to speak of as beautiful. My younger sister, who arrived two years later, once daringly asked my mother what menopause was like, and she replied she had no idea as she was too busy looking after her.

In her final days I would sit with her, rubbing her arthritic hands, marvelling at their leathery feel, kneading them as she had taught me to knead her bread dough daily, as she told me stories of making bread on the small farm where she grew up, how when the yeast plant (as she called it, and what today would be called a sourdough starter)—you—she used this pronoun, so I guess it meant her, and it sounded an adventure the way she spoke of it—*you* would have to go from farm to farm to see if you could get a little of somebody else's yeast plant to make your bread.

Making bread was my mother's way back to her past. She never really left the embattled northwest coast farm of her childhood, dressing until the end of her days like the impoverished farmer her father was until her clothes fell apart, still baking bread daily, still saving dripping and eating it on her toast with relish, still eating leftovers off the plates of others when dinner was finished, still fearful of what she termed *waste*.

Strong and forceful and proud as she was, she had no confidence whatsoever outside of the home. Eating what others had left was part of her pride inside the home. She tried to demonstrate her willingness, her strength, her pride in her humility. But there was some abasement about it I hated. Some surrender, some acceptance of a profound wrong that was too vast to have a name.

To this day I cannot eat food off another plate. I see it as scraps. My mother didn't. And to this day I can only remember my mother as fiercely living her code of love and loyalty in a world and a time and a place that allowed her so little else, this strong, remarkable woman who couldn't be who she really was. And yet how I wished she hadn't done that.

6

Hands impressed her. Some people had *clever* hands while others were *all fingers*. Her beloved father was *good with his hands*. She used the word *clever* in its archaic sense of meaning good with your hands, possessing practical skills. Straying too far into the world of ideas was beset with dilemmas and even dangers. Good hands made for a good life but too many ideas made only for trouble.

Her hands were capable of other things—they could, when she was angry, which was not infrequently for she was fiery and impetuous, deliver what was called a whack—a resounding blow from the open hand, or slamming the flat of a kitchen knife hard across the back of a hand or, in a wild flailing, hitting one or another of us with a wooden jam spoon (the intimidatingly large, as well as the small soup variety) which she sometimes broke on us. On one memorable occasion she chased one of my brothers around the lounge room with an iron fire poker trying to *crown him*—hit him in the head—with it. None of us was in any more doubt that she intended to hit him as hard as she could if she had her chance as we were united in our judgement that he had deserved it and brought it on himself. When we got too much for her she simply uttered one word: *scram*.

And if you were foolish enough not to do so immediately, or simply weren't paying attention, then it was felt you had it coming.

Once, running a stick along the railings of a wrought-iron fence in Macquarie Street after visiting the ear specialist, I almost fell to the pavement when my mother slapped my head hard from behind. "Don't show off" was all she said as I regained my footing and tried not to cry. I thought there had been a misunderstanding. I said I wasn't showing off. I couldn't explain that the rhythm, the vibration passing from stick to body, the creation of all that syncopated noise, were interesting and pleasurable.

"What do you call that nonsense with the stick then?" she said. "Don't show off."

And I understood something fundamental: never draw attention to yourself. It was the lesson she had absorbed and lived by. But it was no law, just a formula for survival when you are one of the weak. And she, the strongest of women, had subjugated herself to this oppressive lie that only served to keep her among the weak.

One day, as an old woman, she broke down in her kitchen while talking with me.

"I am so sorry," she kept saying; I had no idea what she meant. I took her hand, once so strong and sometimes so frightening, now arthritic and affectionate.

"I used to hit you," she finally sobbed.

She was overcome with remorse. Tears in the old do not roll, they catch and stall in the lines and furrows of the face, spot-glossing the price paid for time. She could not understand why she had ever done such a thing. Nor did she believe what I said: that it never worried me, that I never thought of those acts as violent. In the context of those times when I had friends who were thrashed with jug cords and belts it seemed to be of no note. We were many, and we lived together, and she ran the house for us all, her six kids, her demanding mother, her sick husband. She loved us fiercely. And that is what I remembered as we sat together that morning, her love, her hand in mine.

7

When I found my childhood home in Rosebery with the BBC crew, the small wooden bungalow was enshrouded in rainforest plants, and beginning, as everything did and does in that world, to give itself over to the undertow of the natural world. Behind a manfern's fronds I found the window of what had been the children's bedroom, and to the left of that window my head had once lain on a pillow as our mother read to us. Sometimes she would have to stop because she couldn't be heard over the rain. We would wait until the squall abated, wondering what happened next to Moley, who had discovered the joys of leaving his subterranean home and living on a river, or Peter the Pirate who in his toy boat made his way down the river to the wide-open sea. Both, I see now, are children's versions of a road novel, full of joy, fleeting encounters, underpinned by the liberating necessity of departure. Peter's journey is really a picture-book *Odyssey,* the wide-open sea his Ithaca, while Moley learns that you can never return.

Yet sometimes we do.

And now it is not Ratty or Peter, nor Cisco and Pancho, but me and my sister and most of all my mother and father who briefly shape out of the static and rain only to recede back into vaporous memory when I reach out for them. It remains for me to invent what has happened in order to hold them close a little longer. But almost immediately everything starts crumbling into confusions that muddle sweet, salted roast mutton scraps on buttery toast we ate for Sunday breakfast with a spoon of foul-tasting grenadine-coloured medicine for worms that our mother chased us around the house trying to get us to swallow; the joys of childhood with the growing pain and bewilderment of those years as my deafness grew worse, as people became harder to comprehend, and I struggled to be understood with my increasingly poor language. Only when we moved to Hobart was my condition correctly diagnosed and my hearing rectified with a series of minor operations. Without Rosebery, without its alcoholic doctor who failed to diagnose my condition leading to compounding complications, I would never have known that strange nether world of isolation and pain I did in those years of deafness, when slowly I gathered that people thought I was simple.

As you learn that you are written upon you learn to read people. My hearing difficulties took me away from the spoken word where to this day I stumble and mispronounce and cover and panic and suffer, in consequence, attacks of shyness, and took me into the world of the written word where I found ease and joy. I found myself on the page, not as one but as many.

I learnt to draw on myself and invent other worlds in which I increasingly lived, creating friends, places, stories in which it was possible to live fully as the many people and things I might be rather than the incomprehensible child the world increasingly dismissed.

Nor would I have learnt to pay close attention to the small, the insignificant and the seemingly obvious: the smell of rain, the levitational power of light; the comfort of touching moss and the way water sometimes moves in circles. Nor would I have understood that the world exists even when we cannot communicate any of it; that it has its own worth and truth that is not less for not being noticed, that an embarrassment of words does not make something special, far less real, to say nothing of the extraordinary power of small kindnesses. Freed from the opinions and orthodoxies imposed by the language of others, the world came to me as irreducible revelations that stayed with me ever after.

8

Nearing the end in her little room in the nursing home, I would often take my mother's hand, pushing its leathery, crusty skin folds back and forth. I later wrote in a novel of a character who, similarly sitting next to their dying mother, finds some hand cream and rubs it into the back of her mother's hand. I never did that. I made it up. I made it up regretting that so much of my thought had gone into my writing a novel about loving people around you and so little into loving the people around me. Maybe that's what the past is. Making it up so we can keep moving along. Perhaps the past is where we are going and have never been.

My mother had asked me if she and my father might come and live with me. Begged me. It was when, in her nineties, she understood they would soon have to move into a home unless some other arrangement could be made. And I, who had always thought I would say yes, said no. I had my reasons. I could not have worked and been the full-time carer my parents needed. I could have been that carer and forsaken work. But was that even possible? Perhaps, perhaps not. There is no memory without shame.

9

My mother was three days dying. Her nursing home bedroom and the corridor outside it filled with relatives and friends. She was ninety-five, had had several strokes, was very weak, and her mind was sometimes confused. Her body had shrivelled away, her face had lost its softer features and reduced to something elemental if not immediately familiar. Yet dying became her.

Each visitor would bend down close to her head, which she could no longer lift, and they would lean in close to her lips, close to her mouth, which could no longer speak in more than short whispers. There was a strange energy about the darkened room full of people that was also a feeling outside of time, as there is also sometimes with rooms in which babies are being born. She wanted a priest and a priest was found. He read the last rites. The rites were her way of saying in front of us whom she loved more than life itself that she was leaving it, and she was able to convey that most terrible news both to herself and to us, that she was now going and that it was all right, that it was her time and her choice.

She grew weaker, yet each new arrival delighted her. She had always loved what she called a hooley, a gathering of family and friends, and her dying was to be her last, greatest hooley. More people came, making their way around those who were sitting squashed up next to each other on the floor, squeezing past those standing with their backs to the wall, whispering apologies, exchanging smiles, greetings, even jokes, until they found themselves next to where her shrunken, drawn face lay on what seemed an overly large pillow. Her face was transfigured into something smaller, stronger, almost raptor-like in its dignity and ferocious pride. Only her hands remained as they were. Now, though, they seemed oversized and too overtly strong when attached to her frail, emaciated, dying body.

She would gesture with her right index finger, so very slowly hooking it back and forth, a signal for the next visitor to come to her. She was too exhausted to even move her head by this stage, but as each newcomer leant down her face would open into a smile that was unbearable to witness in its love and gratitude.

The strokes had left her mind often addled and confused. Yet in her final days she found some unexpected new clarity and, with it, a grace. Each new arrival would introduce themselves and wait for the blessing of her ever-quieter voice. After a moment or two she would somehow find it within herself to say something meaningful to each person who came to say farewell. It was always apposite, a strange and unexpected blessing, and after, each person would step away consoled, comforted and not a little astonished.

Since the Franklin I had been terrified of death but here was her gift to us: that dying, as well as sometimes being terrifying, can, if you were lucky and if you knew grace, also be serene. It is a cliché but in this case true: her dying over those three days was one of the most beautiful things I ever saw.

Finally, after a long coughing jag, she struggled to clear her throat. It was clear that she wanted to say something to everyone.

The room quietened. She smiled.

"Thank you all for coming," she said. "I have had a lovely time."

Her hands, which is what I for some reason remember above all of her, had grown cold. She never spoke again. That evening she died.

10

My mother and my father—

11

My mother and my father, different as they were, he with his reserve, she with her passion; he with his distance, she with her engagement. My mother and father, born to poverty and grateful to the point of astonishment that their children had all lived, that they did not want for food and knew pain only rarely, fully accepted the unequal terms on which the world had come to them. For they were alive and lived. On only one matter would they not budge: the inviolability of their souls that they somehow kept beyond corruption.

My illiterate grandfather understood something fundamental. "If you don't have principles," he once told my father, "you may as well jump off the end of the jetty." Inscribe that above every parliament and board room entrance. "Crayfish to no man," Tom, my father's brother and a labourer all his life, once said. Tattoo that on every politician's and journalist's forehead.

Tom died playing darts in the St. Leonards Hotel. Great-uncle Babes used to play piano at the St. Leonards Hotel as well as at Ma Dwyer's. One night there was a brawl and his songbook was torn in the melee and scattered over the floor. Babes—Babes because he was the thirteenth of thirteen children—well-primed himself, grabbed random pages off the floor and continued playing seamlessly, passing from "Home on the Range" on the ripped left-hand page to "Beautiful Dreamer" on the torn right without missing a note.

My mother and father had a similar gift, of stitching together torn fragments into some harmony amidst the melee of daily life. My mother and my father in their stories and jokes, in their generosity and kindness to others, asserted the necessary illusion their lives might mean something in the endless tumult of this meaningless universe. For them to live, love had to exist, the love they valued above all things; they lived that love and they fought for that love and defended that love. With the passing of time this illusion became their hard-won truth. It was a form of magic and they the magicians.

In my vanity, I had always thought of them as

naïve. Only now writing these words do I finally see the naïveté was all mine.

12

And so I stood, an adult outside my childhood bedroom, manfern fronds in hand, as though I could see inside, as if I were listening to her once more, teaching me the word *hospital,* which like so many other words I could not pronounce, making me sound it out syllable by syllable, patiently and kindly repeating the sounds for days on end until I could master them. *Ho—spit—al, ho—spit—al,* and me, a six-year-old boy, struggling to repeat it, unable to say it, but knowing somehow we would make it to the next sound together. And all that love, and all the enduring power of that love, I was at that moment so many years later unable to express, and I was once more without words as the fern fronds swept back and resumed the perpetual unravelling that is their particular wisdom. I walked back to where the crew had set up the camera and set about pretending to answer questions that had no meaning to me, making sounds that made no sense, as it is and was and will forever be, lost again in the river of time.

Eight

1

"You see now," Einstein said over iced tea to his former student and old friend when Leo Szilard visited after Hiroshima, "that the ancient Chinese were right. It is not possible to foresee the results of what you do. The only wise thing to do is to take no action—to take absolutely no action."

But Szilard, although a corpulent man who loathed physical labour, was incapable of inaction. Having been pivotal in creating a new world founded on terror he would now seek to dismantle it, his seeming model once more *The World Set Free,* in which Szilard had read of how Leblanc sought to bring together "all the rulers of the world and unify them. He wrote innumerable letters, he sent messages, he went on desperate journeys, he enlisted whatever support he could find . . . through the terrible autumn of the last [nuclear] wars this persistent little visionary in spectacles must have seemed rather like a hopeful canary twittering during a thunderstorm."

If by nature more a volatile owl than a hopeful canary, Szilard nevertheless now found a new destiny echoing that of Leblanc. Believing that nuclear war could be prevented if the world's scientists banded together and wrested control of the bomb away from states, politicians and generals, he became a protean figure in the postwar, reshaping variously as an agitator, writer, biologist, inventor and high-level lobbyist. Selfless and unflagging, Szilard launched movements, councils and societies, many of which were to play a significant role in alerting the world to the dangers of nuclear warfare, seeking arms control and civilian control of nuclear weaponry.

His activism made him famous, and though he never won the Nobel Prize for physics, many eminent scientists and Nobel laureates believed he deserved it, while others argued he should win the Nobel Peace Prize for his attempts to stop nuclear war. For his part, Szilard joked he deserved the Nobel Peace Prize for failing to discover nuclear fission in the 1930s, which he believed, not without good reason, would have inevitably led to a nuclear-armed Nazi Germany. Yet, in a torment worthy of the ancient Greeks, as his fame grew his influence paradoxically waned, his ideas and influence fell out of favour, and his hope for a Wellsian world government faded. Where Leblanc succeeded, Szilard failed.

He continued to live out of hotel rooms, using the foyers and lobbies as his office for waging his ever more quixotic campaign that seemed only slightly less preposterous than a reality that saw the world edging closer to nuclear destruction. Caught in the cruel vortex of his own creation, Szilard, unlike Leblanc, could not stop the terrifying dynamic of postwar nuclear proliferation and brinkmanship. As the years passed, there were only more and more bombs and more countries with them, while Leo Szilard grew fatter and the bombs bigger.

2

In his final years, he returned to the form that had first led him to the bomb: fiction. He wrote a story in the manner of Wells's great works. Presented as a dry history written in the future, it told of a pod of dolphins kept in a tank in a Viennese research institute. Discovered to be more intelligent than humans, the dolphins suggest experiments for the institute's scientists that win their human handlers successive Nobel Prizes. The dolphins next reshape world affairs by using their growing influence with the scientists to end the risk from nuclear war and bring about world peace.

The story cannot help but seem a counterfactual autobiography, the dolphins a cetacean reimagining of Szilard's Bund thirty years on, a Wellsian elite of scientists reconceived. Szilard, who had seen his rational ideas constantly defeated by an irrational world remade the irrational world as one in which rational dolphins triumphed. With this reverse alchemy, an aspect of Wells's fiction that failed to transform into a reality transformed back into fiction.

The story was published in *The Voice of the Dolphins* in April 1961, a book that included several other stories by Leo Szilard. Six months later, on 30 October 1961, as if to mock him and all who thought nuclear weapons could be brought under rational control, the USSR detonated the Tsar Bomba in the Russian Arctic. It was the largest nuclear explosion in history.

3

The flash of light was visible more than 2,500 kilometres away, its pressure wave blowing windows out as far away as Norway and Finland. Everything within a hundred kilometres was severely damaged and everything within a sixty-kilometre radius was destroyed. The equivalent of fifty-seven million tons of TNT, the Tsar Bomba was 3,300 times more powerful than the Hiroshima bomb and ten times more powerful than all the munitions expended during the Second World War. Tellingly, terrifyingly, Tsar Bomba was detonated at only half the blast power of which it was capable.

By this time Szilard's naïve ideal of a Wellsian elite of scientists had thinned to little more than a hollow vanity, Szilard believing that "besides being cleverer than congressmen, scientists . . . have integrity and purity." And yet because of their complicity with the bomb, scientists were now seen in the public's eye as hopelessly corrupted, more questionable than deranged generals, more dangerous than unprincipled politicians. And this too was, in no small part, Leo Szilard's unintended legacy.

4

Thirty years earlier, H. G. Wells had been given a personally guided tour by the Nobel Prize–winning chemist Irving Langmuir around General Electric's famed research facilities at Schenectady in New York State, where Edison had perfected the light bulb. Langmuir pitched Wells a story idea about a form of ice, the smallest piece of which could freeze whole oceans. Wells turned the idea down.

But Langmuir's assistant at the time, Bernard Vonnegut, a scientist working with Langmuir on attempts to control the weather, never forgot it. After the war, Bernard got his brother, a former POW who had survived the firebombing of Dresden, a job as a publicist at General Electric. One day Bernard told him Langmuir's idea.

During 1962, in the wake of Tsar Bomba, as the world came perilously close to global nuclear war with the Cuban Missile Crisis, Kurt Vonnegut transformed Langmuir's rejected idea into one of his most celebrated novels, *Cat's Cradle,* in which this new idea of scientists not as moral leaders but as amoral monsters was given its most potent literary expression. A tale about a world destroyed by human stupidity made manifest by a scientist, he also made use of Langmuir himself as the model for the fictional Dr. Felix Hoenikker, a scientist who, in Vonnegut's words, "isn't interested in people." The fictional Hoenikker is the discoverer of ice nine, a form of ice that can instantly freeze anything it touches, from people to oceans, in a form of chain reaction. Hoenikker was previously one of the "fathers" of the atom bomb.

"After the thing went off, after it was a sure thing that America could wipe out a city with just one bomb," Vonnegut wrote, "a scientist turned to Father and said, 'Science has now known sin.' And do you know what Father said? He said, 'What is sin?'"

Vonnegut begins with his narrator planning to write a book called *The Day the World Ended* about what "important Americans" had done the day Thomas Ferebee pulled his lever and the bomb fell on Hiroshima, and finishes six months after the world has more or less ended for all living things save a few ants and a handful of humans.

Perhaps, inevitably, when anyone faces the apocalypse, the example of the Tasmanian Aboriginal people comes up. In Vonnegut's telling in *Cat's Cradle*, they were "hunted for sport" by the first English settlers "who were convicts." The Tasmanian example is the ur-story of the end of the world, much imitated and never rivalled.

5

Cat's Cradle was rapturously reviewed in the *New York Times* by Terry Southern, who was at the time co-writing a film with Stanley Kubrick called *Dr. Strangelove*, in which Peter Sellers's titular character is the apotheosis of the mad scientist. Dr. Strangelove took inspiration from Szilard's close friends and fellow Hungarians Edward Teller and John von Neumann, as well as the Nazi-cum-American rocket scientist Wernher von Braun. In the movie, Dr. Strangelove is responsible for the Doomsday Machine, which was inspired by another idea of Leo Szilard's. Originating as an illustration of where the arms race might lead, Szilard in a 1950 radio broadcast had come up with the idea of the terrifying—and technically possible—notion of the Doomsday Bomb: a cobalt bomb, which could kill all life on the planet.

In an inspired improvisation, Sellers borrowed a glove Kubrick wore when handling hot studio lights. He has Strangelove present as though afflicted by his own gloved hand, giving Nazi salutes and constantly seeking to strangle his own neck. Strangelove has to battle with his uncontrollable hand as the human and irrational comically, continually, assert themselves over the controlled and rational.

Dr. Strangelove was released in January 1964. Four months later Szilard died knowing not dolphins saving the world but rather a madman seeking to strangle himself with his own gloved hand. The last of his paradoxical legacies was that he—an exemplar of the Wellsian ideal of scientists as noble saviours—had unintentionally helped create the opposite image of scientists: that of dehumanised, crippled minds without a conscience, creatures of the darkly irrational.

In their gallows humour and fatal despair, both *Cat's Cradle* and *Dr. Strangelove* are as distant from Wells's optimism as Earth is from Mars, with Vonnegut's Hoenikker and Sellers's Strangelove as removed from Wells's enlightened scientists as the Tsar Bomba is from a firecracker.

Thus do love stories that begin with a kiss in front of a bookcase and continue in baths and traffic lights end: with Tsar Bomba's explosion spreading into a sixty-seven-kilometre-high mushroom cloud looking, according to one witness, as "if the earth was killed."

6

Not long after Andrei Sakharov's greatest triumph, which saw him embraced by Khrushchev in front of the USSR's Politburo, the principal Russian physicist behind the Tsar Bomba, often hailed as the father of the

Russian hydrogen bomb, read one of Szilard's stories published in *The Voice of the Dolphins.* It was called "My Trial as a War Criminal."

Szilard had written it in 1947. In the story, Russia had conquered the United States. Szilard finds himself arrested and tried as a war criminal, charged with inducing the United States to develop nuclear weapons in 1939 and "having contributed to the war crime of dropping an atomic bomb on Hiroshima." The evidence is irrefutable, his defence—that he sought to prevent the bomb being used—rejected.

Szilard's story spoke to Sakharov's own growing doubts. Deeply affected by it, Sakharov showed the story to fellow physicist Viktor Adamsky.

"A number of us discussed it," Adamsky later wrote. Although Szilard and his fellow physicists who are similarly charged are innocent, neither "they nor their lawyers could make up a cogent proof of their innocence," Adamsky continued. "We were amazed by this paradox. You can't get away from the fact that we were developing weapons of mass destruction. We thought it was necessary . . . But still the moral aspect of it would not let Andrei Dmitrievich [Sakharov] and some of us live in peace."

At its beginning the atom bomb was far more a continuation of the grotesquery of modern war than a departure from it. When asked about his decision to drop the bomb, Truman, a former artillery officer, once answered, "It was just the same as getting a bigger gun than the other fellow had to win a war, and that's what it was used for. Nothing else but an artillery weapon."

Sakharov, following Szilard, understood that no gun, no matter how big, threatened the future of humanity. Nuclear weapons did. And in creating them and understanding what they meant he had a moral responsibility to speak out against them. Along the way he became the USSR's most famous dissident.

"His message was unequivocal: there is only one way to avoid a life of lies," his friend and fellow dissident Natan Sharansky wrote of Sakharov. "In order to be truly free, you must speak your mind."

And so, once more, a disappointing reality was reinvented as a fiction that metamorphosed into an unexpected new reality.

7

Szilard's dolphins, brilliant creatures, come to understand maths and science completely and grow bored. Only US politics piques their interest because it defies understanding. And what was US politics or any politics for that matter but the irrational expressed as a system? Perhaps only Szilard's dolphins could finally answer the question that Leo Szilard's life raises: if despair is rational why was hope the very essence of Leo Szilard?

When he was dying Szilard simply said he did

his best. He never stopped trying. He never ceased looking for what he termed the narrow margin of hope, no matter how often it proved elusive. That he failed makes his struggle no less poignant. The example of his life remains: a man who always thought science existed within a web of morality. Science's achievements had to be constantly tested against the reality of human beings and yield to what we are, or we would be consumed and possibly even destroyed by them.

8

Thomas Ferebee felt justified in his part in the destruction of Hiroshima and its people: after all, how many more would have died if the bomb had not been dropped? In July 1945, the American Secretary of War, Henry L. Stimson, commissioned a study on the human cost of an invasion of Japan. It estimated between 1.7 million and four million Allied casualties with 400,000 to 800,000 dead and between five and ten million Japanese dead. So many Purple Hearts (awarded to US soldiers wounded or killed in combat) were manufactured in preparation for the invasion and its expected feats of death—some half a million—that the stockpile has not been exhausted to this day, many wars and nearly eighty years later.

Japanese estimates were higher, with the vice-chief of the Imperial Japanese Navy, Vice Admiral Takijirō Ōnishi, predicting up to twenty million Japanese deaths.

The grand slaughter was being prepared for on every side: biological weapons were also under active consideration and General Douglas MacArthur readied stockpiles of phosgene, mustard gas, and cyanogen chloride close to the front line in the Mariana Islands and ensured the US Chemical Warfare Service units were trained in their use. When it came to which weapon of mass destruction, the atom bomb was simply the final choice.

If there is no precise statistic to measure Hiroshima, nor can it be pretended that there is some moral calculus to death. There is no equation of horrors. Everyone knows of the victims of the first atomic bomb; few know of the Death Railway, whose dead number (in the typically imprecise way of evil) between 100,000 and 250,000 human beings. While the world still grieves for the dead of Hiroshima, outside Japan who grieves for the firebombing of Tokyo, which saw perhaps even more die from conventional bombs than the first atomic bomb—an estimated 100,000 victims? Which is the greater war crime? Who do we remember and who do we forget? Thomas Ferebee or Leo Szilard? A failed actress who makes a stolen stage name her destiny as a writer, or a successful actor with a gloved hand whose screen name becomes a synonym for mad evil while his own name fades from memory? If Thomas Ferebee releases a lever at 8:15 a.m., says, "Bomb away!," and a bomb falls six miles before exploding, how many people need to die in order that you might read this book?

9

Forever after, Thomas Ferebee was asked how he felt about bombing Hiroshima. No one ever asked Thomas Ferebee how he felt about taking part in the first USAAF daylight raid on German-occupied Europe three years earlier. Tasked with destroying the Rouen railyards, half the bombs dropped by the raiding aircraft missed their target, killing fifty-two civilians and wounding 120 more. One Frenchman returned to his home to find it destroyed. At the morgue he discovered among many others the corpses of his parents and his son, naked, still bleeding, with only their socks left on their bodies. Of his daughter no trace was ever found.[8]

The raid was deemed a success that "far exceeded in accuracy any previous high-altitude bombing." Though a demonstrable nonsense, it was used to justify an intensification of aerial bombing. Precision aerial bombing was always a misnomer in search of a justification. Subsequent Allied bombing of France killed, according to one historian, 57,000 French civilians. Estimates of German civilian dead from Allied bombing vary between 300,000 and 600,000.

Nor did anyone ever ask Thomas Ferebee how he felt about taking part in the carpet bombing of Vietnam twenty years later, which he did as a USAF observer. During that war the Americans and their allies dropped on Vietnam, Laos and Cambodia more than double the entirety of bombs it dropped in the Second World War—some 7.5 million tons of ordnance. It remains the largest aerial bombardment in history. Outside the countries that suffered it is largely forgotten.

Little Boy is generally accepted to have exploded with a force equivalent to 15,000 tons of TNT. However, a major postwar US government report, the Strategic Bombing Survey, analysing the effect of aerial bombing in the Second World War, estimated that the same blast and fire effect of the Little Boy explosion could have been achieved with 2,100 tons of conventional bombs. In other words, the bombing of Vietnam can be calculated as the equivalent of either 500 Hiroshima bombs (at 15,000 tons) or, using the Strategic Bombing Survey figures, the equivalent of 3,571 Hiroshima bombs (at 2,100 tons). It is impossible to accurately quantify in a war that saw more than three million die, of whom two million were civilians, how many died from aerial bombing. We remember Hiroshima. Who, other than the Vietnamese, remembers the Vietnamese dead? Other than the Cambodians, the Cambodian dead? The Laotians, the Laotian dead?

But then, who remembers a vanished daughter?

10

After Sanyo-Onada City and the night of the hostess bar I returned to Tokyo. There I met a man who had been a Japanese Army medical orderly at Hintok, the POW camp on the Death Railway where my father had also been. He described arriving there at night and walking past the funeral pyres on which were burning the cholera dead. Around the fires of flesh and bamboo were pitiful naked skeletons crawling in the mud. These, he told me, were the Australian POWS.

We met at a tearoom, a small space up a stairwell of an anonymous office block. There was a large window at one end of its narrow room. It was a place without charm, whose function was its function and no more.

It looked, he said of the camp, like a Buddhist hell.

I asked if he helped them.

He said he didn't.

I asked if as a medical man he did not feel it was his duty to help the sick and the suffering.

"You have to understand," he said, and he said it as though commenting on the quality or otherwise of his green tea, "we did not see them as human beings."

The green tea came in small cups. It was very hard to swallow.

He told me the Australians were bad with their hygiene. The Japanese took hot baths. The Australians did not.

This seemed to explain things. I said nothing in reply.

"You understand?" he said.

I said I did.

I paid for his tea and taxi home. Nothing could have prepared me for what was to happen next.

11

I had arranged to meet another ex-guard later that day. I knew nothing about him. He had nothing to do with my father. He had just been one of thousands of guards who had worked on the pharaonic project that was the Death Railway with its hundreds of thousands of slaves. While travelling on a train to the outer suburbs of Tokyo where I was to meet him in the offices of a taxi company owned by his son, I had googled him to discover that he had only reverted to his original Korean name in recent times. His former Japanese name, Kakurai Hiromura, the name he had used during the war, that name I knew. He had been the Ivan the Terrible of my father's camp, the man the Australians called the Lizard.

He is the only man I have ever heard my father—a gentle, peaceful man—speak of with violent intent. My father told me he had a dream of which he was ashamed—and I cannot tell you how out of character it was—and in that dream they captured the Lizard and bayoneted him and tied him up with his entrails.

Lee Hak-rae was sentenced to death for war crimes after the war. Later, his death sentence was commuted to life imprisonment and in 1956 he was released in a general amnesty.

12

Lee Hak-rae was a dignified, gracious and generous old man. He did his best to answer my questions politely and thoughtfully. He had no recollection of violence. Perhaps it happened, he said. But he never saw it. He gave the impression of being sincere. I wondered if perhaps he had forgotten or he had decided to forget or it had receded from his mind, or if perhaps as an old man many things had vanished. Yet when I asked him about other aspects of that period in his life—his life in Korea before becoming a prison guard, his training by the Japanese, he was surprisingly full of precise details.

Violent face slapping—known as *binta*—was the immediate form of punishment in the camps, doled out frequently and viciously. There was often no discernible reason for the violence. Prisoners could be slapped until they were unconscious. Sometimes POWs were lined up in two rows and made to slap the man opposite them. The slapping would go on until one man fell. Anyone who was thought to be feigning their blows would be beaten by the guards.

Of course, he told me, he knew about binta. But that was just for discipline.

I asked him to slap me. I asked him to slap me as hard as he could.

My request was curious, even perverse. I still don't understand why I asked. I tried to meet each witness without emotion, so that I would be open to everything they said and were, and not to prosecute, nor to judge. But perhaps I wanted him to know I knew. Perhaps, in spite of myself, I wasn't without emotion. Perhaps I wanted him to know the past had returned, that, finally, it always returns. Or I wanted him to know I couldn't be hurt as my father had been hurt. Perhaps I thought I needed to know what it was like waiting for the blow, how it might snap your head around, how you might seek to ride the blow while accepting it. But to be truthful, to this day I still really don't understand why I asked.

The old man took some persuasion. Finally, we stood up, facing each other. He angled his body so that the force of his torso was behind the blow, slightly crooked his arm to buffer the blow, and cupped his hand to maximise the blow. It was evident that even if he had forgotten his violence his wasted muscles and withered body had not.

He hit me three times.

Of his slaps, I recall only how clean and dry the skin of his aged hand was as it struck me. It smelt of precisely nothing.

On the third blow, the taxi office began to shake and toss violently, like a dinghy in a wild sea. The whole building reeled around me. Folders fell from shelves as cupboards rocked. A long row of wildly swinging car keys began an ethereal jingling. I thought I had finally gone mad, that the whole trip to Japan, the novel I had been writing for over a decade and yet couldn't write, had finally cracked my mind.

But in one of those coincidences in which reality delights but fiction—for fear of being unrealistic—is never permitted, a 7.3 Richter scale earthquake had hit Tokyo.

I had never experienced an earthquake and was too ignorant to be frightened. But Lee Hak-rae had. For the half a minute that room swayed, I saw that he was very frightened. I saw too that wherever evil is, it wasn't in that room with me and that terrified old man gripping the table edge as if it were flotsam and he was drowning.

13

When I went to leave he made a show of presenting me with an envelope of money to give to my father. It was yen to the value of twenty dollars. As if in a dream I stared at it unable to move. I felt so many things but above all I felt powerless. For what good was done, what wrong righted, what dead man resurrected, by giving offence? And so I accepted the gift politely, knowing I would never give it to my father nor tell my father about it, feeling that I had somehow traded away something invaluable and beyond any price. I hated the feel of that envelope, the deep sense of complicity and shame it summoned up in me. I threw it in a bin as soon as I left, fearing it had some power over me, some magical hold, but the feelings were not so easily disposed of. The unwelcome sense of shared guilt. I felt as if covered in filth.

14

Japan was on its knees by August 1945, its people close to starvation. The villagers around my father's camp were reduced to living on little more than roots. For the slave labourers there was even less. The winter had been exceptionally cold. My father lost the belief he would survive. His condition grew so pitiful that even among the pitiful he was for a time excused from work in the coal mine. He was put on light duties carrying the human waste from the toilet trenches to a vegetable garden up the hill—called *yama* in Japanese—heavy buckets of filth slung on a bamboo pole carried by two men. The task was known as carrying shit up the yama.

One day an English POW refused to carry his end of the bamboo pole on the grounds he wouldn't lower himself to work with a half-caste such as my father. Here, at the end of their world, a nonsensical distinction between slaves still mattered to the Englishman. To the end of his days, that memory of the Englishman refusing to carry shit up the yama with him still made my father smile.

Among the many fated to die in any invasion were the 32,000 Allied POWs who had been transported to

Japan as a slave labour force. It was widely expected that the POWs would be mass murdered on invasion or, at best, used as human shields.

None of this is an argument for the bombing of Hiroshima. All of it is an argument against war, an argument that can never be won but must never stop being made. Tragedy is sometimes understood as the conflict of one good against another. A more nuanced form of this idea is that tragedy is the conflict between what is perceived to be a lesser evil against what is perceived to be a greater evil. Tragedy exerts its hold upon our imaginations because it reminds us that justice is an illusion. Hiroshima is the great tragedy of our age from which we continue to seek understanding and yet can never understand.

"Bomb away!" Thomas Ferebee said, the silver-plated B-29 banked up and away and shortly after he fell asleep and slept the rest of the twelve-hour flight back to their airbase on Tinian Island. In his retirement he liked growing roses. "Bomb away!" Thomas Ferebee said and Thomas Ferebee is about to say and Thomas Ferebee is forever saying, his body perennially glowing with all the innumerable innocent forever passing through him.

15

My father, who wasn't a man for such things, rang within a few hours of my returning home from Japan.

He wanted to know what had happened. He was ninety-seven, frail, but his mind was still good. I told him how the Japanese people had been unfailingly kind and generous, and how, amazingly, I had met with some guards who had been at his camps, including the Lizard.

And what did they say? he asked.

I thought of the earthquake. Of Mr. Sato curling inwards. Of the near empty hostess bar. Of Lee Hak-rae gripping a table as the world rolled around him.

I said that they talked in detail about all of their lives except the camps where details seemed to elude them, but that I felt nevertheless that they carried shame, and how each one had expressed their sorrow and apologies for what had happened and asked me to pass them on to my father. That much was true. It was also probably untrue. And yet it was as much as I could say with any honesty.

Of Australians being dirty I said nothing. Of Lee Hak-rae's twenty dollars of yen I said nothing.

My father stopped talking. After some time, he said he had to go, and hung up.

Later that day, my father lost all memory of his time in the POW camps. Before I had left for Japan he had lost memory of the violence. Then he had lost memory of the mud which had so tormented them all during the hell of the Speedo. Now, though, everything had gone. He knew in an abstract way—as you know you have been in the womb—that he had been in the camps, but no memory of those years remained. And yet his memory before and after the camps remained strong.

It was as though he were finally free.

In the end all that remained to him was an idea of love. He had spent a lifetime pondering that short, terrible period of his life and through some slow reduction had distilled it down to one idea, one emotion, one truth: love.

And I realise writing this that memory is as much an act of creation as it is of testimony, and that one without the other is a tree without its trunk, wings without a bird, a book without its story.

16

I wrote a novel seeking to understand these things. To resolve them. For the time I spent writing it I felt that the writing was a way of divining the undivinable. Only when I finished I realised I understood nothing.

17

Who loves longer?

18

My father was ill, and I was with him early that morning. How's the book going? he asked. I told him it was finally done. That night he died.

Nine

1

After the great success of *The Time Machine* in 1895, the young H. G. Wells turned out in astonishingly quick succession five "scientific romances"—as science fiction was then called—in three years, culminating in 1898 in perhaps his most enduring work, *The War of the Worlds,* in which an ancient civilisation of octopus-like creatures from Mars invades Earth with extreme violence. *The War of the Worlds* is science fiction's great ur-story.

Wells's novel combined a fashion for "invasion" stories with inventions of such startling originality that it became the bedrock of much of twentieth-century popular culture. His tale of an extraterrestrial army, the motives of which are as incomprehensible as its technology is fatal, popularised the idea of superior nonhuman civilisations from other planets with a term that became commonplace for such an alien life form: Martians.

2

"But where are they?" Enrico Fermi asked a table of fellow physicists half a century later when chatting about the now much-discussed possibility of intelligent life from other planets. Fermi, *the architect of the atomic bomb,* next asked a question that became celebrated as the Fermi Paradox: if aliens were so likely to exist given the infinite plenitude of planets, why had no compelling evidence ever been found in the universe for any form of higher life?

Leo Szilard had the answer.

"They are among us," he replied, "but they are called Hungarians."

Szilard's joke led to a label for a phenomenon: he and four other Jewish-Hungarian scientists—renowned for such inexplicable brilliance as to seem otherworldly, speaking an incomprehensible native tongue and an oddly accented English—became known as the Martians.

The joke was adopted by the five—Edward Teller, *the father of the hydrogen bomb,* pointing out that his initials also stood for extraterrestrial. Soon enough they even had a foundation story: three years after the publication of Wells's masterpiece, Martians were said to have come to Earth, not violently to Woking, Surrey, as in Wells's novel, but quietly to Budapest, Hungary, as an advance scout force. When Earth proved unsuitable for colonisation they departed, leaving behind five children conceived with local women. The Martians' children grew up and became brilliant scientists who would, among much else, be in no small part responsible for inventing the atom bomb, with one central to its creation: Leo Szilard.

3

The War of the Worlds had its genesis in the attempted genocide of the Tasmanian Aboriginal people. In a 1920 interview with *Strand* magazine, H. G. Wells attributed the idea of the book to a remark of his brother Frank, to whom he dedicated the novel. They had been talking "of the discovery of Tasmania by the Europeans—a very frightful disaster for the native Tasmanians." "We were walking together through some particularly peaceful Surrey scenery. 'Suppose some beings from another planet were to drop out of the sky suddenly,' said he, 'and begin laying about them here!'"

In the first chapter of *The War of the Worlds,* Wells makes the connection explicit—"Before we judge them [the Martians] too harshly, we must remember what ruthless and utter destruction our own species has wrought, not only upon animals, such as the vanished bison and the dodo, but upon its own inferior races. The Tasmanians, in spite of their human likeness, were entirely swept out of existence in a war of extermination waged by European immigrants, in the space of fifty years. Are we such apostles of mercy as to complain if the Martians warred in the same spirit?"

4

For a time the pale invaders must have seemed to the Tasmanian Aboriginal people as ephemeral as they had at first thought, ghosts revisiting their onetime world, as annoying and as trivial and transitory as distant visiting relatives. But they didn't leave. They kept coming. More and more of them. When the Aboriginal people found themselves being destroyed by simple musket balls and complex disease, by butchery and by treachery, they may have felt, nevertheless, that their verities, their cosmos, their understanding of this world and their place within would endure this murderous nonsense and prevail as it had for forty millennia before.

That wasn't what happened though.

The handful of Tasmanian Aboriginal people who survived the Black War—at most a few hundred—found themselves living in a world that, as well as being intolerable, must have also quickly become unreadable and thus absurd to them. For millennia on millennia, their stories wrote the land and the land wrote them. Whatever ideas, whatever knowledge the first Tasmanians had about the way meaning was bound into the material world of rock and river and sea and fish and tree and grass and bird and animal now meant nothing to the conquerors. Wherever the surviving Aboriginal people went there had once been words, names, practices, ideas, spirits, laws, songs, dances and stories but these were now deemed irrelevant. But if the extermination was not complete, nor was the cataclysm total. Much was lost, but some things endured.

Their island was stolen by the English but, in so doing, the English also stole and destroyed what was sacred. Looked at this way, the temple was the island and the English temple robbers. The word *sacrilege* derives from the same word in Latin, in which it means to steal sacred things. The invasion was a sacrilegious act. Perhaps the gaping absence that haunts contemporary Tasmania is the loss of that sacred world. For we cannot imagine it. If it were imaginable we could not be Australia today. The ensuing enforcement of the great silence, no matter the pain; the violent rage that feels the need over and over in Tasmania to destroy what is unique and beautiful, no matter the loss; all this comes from something deep within us, for which the word *guilt* is inadequate and perhaps even wrong. Could it be that it is the unbearable, intolerable knowledge that a sacred world was profaned? And that what remains of it must be obliterated so no memory remains?

The English invaders frequently noted the great love the first Tasmanians had of their country without understanding its profound roots. They saw this love as the motivation that made their guerrilla war against overwhelming odds so ferocious, effective and long lasting. They did not understand that this love was to prove not so easily vanquished, nor so readily extinguished.

5

The Martian John von Neumann, one of the greatest mathematicians of his age, attributed the Martian phenomenon to the Austro-Hungarian mix of liberalism and feudalism that allowed Jews some avenues for success while keeping them away from power. This provoked "a feeling of extreme insecurity," von Neumann said, making him and his fellow Martians believe that they needed "to produce the unusual or face extinction." Perhaps, for the same reason, Szilard never owned a house and always kept two bags packed, ever ready to flee to the next country.

The Jewish Martians weren't really Martians at all: they were just one more people the real Martians exterminated.

6

If the destruction of the Tasmanian Aboriginal people was apocalyptic it was not total: a few survived that war of extermination (as Wells correctly named it and as colonists at the time called it), and today 30,000 claim descent from a handful of survivors.

But the genocide was not exactly, as Wells had it in his social-Darwinian way, what a species did unto itself. Rather, it was British government policy pursued with determined intent to secure the fertile grassland for the burgeoning business of sheep, the wool of which was a key commodity fuelling Britain's industrial revolution. As in Thomas More's *Utopia,* sheep once more were eating people—though with the aid of muskets, pistols, soldiers, roaming death squads, disease and systematic military organisation committed to their destruction. Looked at this way, the effect was little different from a nuclear explosion because the intent was the same: obliteration. The distance between *The War of the Worlds* and *The World Set Free* is not so great.

The invasion was at once a war of genocide and the creation of a totalitarian slave society in the newly emptied lands. And it was as just such a slave labourer on just such a sheep farm that my great-great-grandfather Thomas Flanagan began his life in Van Diemen's Land, on a plantation called Brickendon on the outskirts of a village called Longford, formerly the kangaroo hunting grounds of the Panniher people.

Less than a mile from where Thomas Flanagan arrived as a convict slave and 110 years later, in the short time between the publication of *The Voice of the Dolphins* and the detonation of Tsar Bomba, I was born on a misty winter's morning. My mother, already dealing with four children, her demanding mother and her sick husband, wept on learning she was pregnant with me, while my father dreamt of watching from inside his coffin the streets of Longford and its staring people pass by him.

7

Tasmania does not begin with a monolithic group of Martians invading and Europeans uniformly benefiting from the conquest. The Martians were the rulers and everyone else the ruled. The term *settler-colonial society* is lazy thinking that hides the inequality on which the new Martian world was built and the pathologies that flow from it, which run deep to this day.

Contemporary observers often commented on the way convictism was another name for slavery. The Tasmanian Aboriginal people understood the social distinction perhaps better than the slaves themselves: they liked to point out that even defeated in war they remained a free people and of a status above that of the convicts, whom they looked down upon as the unfree. That manumission was the likely but not necessary end of a Van Diemonian convict's sentence did not mean it was any less a slave system than that of Rome. That a freed slave might rise did not mean the society was any less unfree. Nor did the shared horror of convict and Aboriginal necessarily lead to solidarity: when in 1832 a group of Aboriginal people was temporarily housed on the floor below convicts in the Macquarie Island penitentiary, the convicts pissed onto them between the floorboards.

On manumission the emancipated convicts were not allowed to return to their homelands but had to stay in the colonies. It was widely observed that they evaded the cities where the authorities ruled, preferring to find a new life in the bush where their ways often came to resemble that of the Aboriginal people with whom they sometimes had children, and these too were hidden from the authorities, their origins obscured and kept secret from the broader world. Some began to eat and live and even dress like Tasmanian Aboriginal people. A 40,000-year-old culture proved itself not so easily destroyed, nor was its ongoing influence restricted only to Aboriginal people. It re-formed and reshaped and, over time, as much as there was a process of colonisation, another river, a far older river, kept flowing, and a reverse process of what we might call indigenisation also occurred, in which the freed convicts and their families and their descendants took on some of the values and mentality of Aboriginal people.

They were becoming something else, though what that something else was none knew because no one named it. They turned it into sly jokes and long stories, they felt it when they made their way through the bush, they heard it in the unique sound the wind makes passing through she-oak groves, they tasted it in the wallaby and crayfish and abalone and scallops they ate, they sensed it in the laughter and griefs of their clannish families, in the way they thought about time and land and home. But no one named it and no one could say it, and everyone claimed to be a Martian though almost no one was.

It was as if it were all finally a matter of question 7, of who loves longer, for white people had begun in some ways to think like black people. Despite themselves, they had begun living in the circles of time with which the Tasmanian Aboriginal people had once marked their island. They were not Aboriginal. Over time many became racist. But nor were they any longer European.

8

By the time he died at the age of ninety-eight my father had few material possessions left other than an armchair, chair and desk in which he had collected various writings precious to him over the years: poems, sayings, quotes, a few pieces he had written, some correspondence. Among these papers my elder sister found a letter from a now-dead cousin on his mother's side written years before about how when they were growing up they were told over and over never to mention outside of the home that their family had black blood. The implication was that our grandmother was of Aboriginal descent.

My father loved discussing interesting letters with his family. He never discussed this letter. The story of covering up Aboriginal pasts was a common one in Tasmania where such behaviour was for some a form of survival. There is no documentation to prove my father's cousin's story is true, but that doesn't make it untrue. It leaves the story as an unanswerable question mark over my family.

We, like many other Tasmanian families, have Aboriginal relatives. But even if our cousin's story were true we would not be Aboriginal. We were not brought up in the Aboriginal culture or an Aboriginal community, far less known the profound racism Aboriginal people endure. But who, then, are we? Why are we? For we, like so many other Tasmanian families, live in the shade of old stories that remain with us along with the new ones that accrue.

Why had our father, nicknamed Nugget as a child after the boot polish label because he was dark, not taken issue with those who accused him as an adult of being "half-caste"? Where had his spiritual beliefs, highly unusual in a man born in 1914, come from?

Experience is but a moment. Making sense of that moment is a life.

9

It is little noted that Franz Kafka remains unrecognised as the leading writer of Tasmania. In his short story "In the Penal Colony," a traveller arrives in an unnamed colony. There the condemned are found guilty without being told what their crime is and given no opportunity to defend themselves. Their punishment is to be chained, gagged and laid in the Harrow—an ingenious machine mounted in glass so that the punishment can be observed from above by a large audience looking down. The bound body of the condemned rotates as their unspoken crime is slowly inscribed by needles working ever deeper into their flesh until in their final agony the condemned realise their crime and die.

I read this story with the shock of horrified recognition.

"White Australians still struggle to come to terms with their colonial past," the English *Independent*—a Martian newspaper—declared in 2009, its Harrow needles beginning their work, inescapable as a man trap, as if the genocide was our invention and not theirs, as though the totalitarian slave system was our choice and not their gulag. How marvellous, to have an empire, reap its robbed riches, and yet etch its colonial failings on the colonised, to write on our bodies that we were the vulgar arriviste, the barbarian, the savage, that their judgement was our crime.

The sorry truth is that the extermination was a Martian project. The sorry truth is that the totalitarian slave system was a Martian project. It's as if the Thousand Year Reich had prevailed and 150 years later blamed the Holocaust on the Jewish survivors. As William

Rees-Mogg, former editor of *The Times* and father of leading English Tory politician Jacob Rees-Mogg, put it in 1998, "The genocide of the Tasmanian Aboriginals . . . was also part of an historic record which brought the benefits of civilisation to a quarter of the world."

If I weary of the enormous Martian condescension, the endless Martian capacity for patronising, the unquestioned Martian superiority, the unending Martian arrogance that is always founded in an equal Martian stupidity and an unrivalled Martian ignorance, it is not because I think they alone are uniquely guilty.

It is because they cannot conceive—as Kafka could—that we all are.

10

The whole truth, the terrible truth, is that the Martians created the System (as it was eerily known and capitalised) in which we as convicts were made to be our own convict-constable, our own convict-flagellator, our own convict-spy and our own convict-hangman, all these posts and positions being filled by convicts. We acted as our own convict-clerks and our own convict-archivists of the System, recording our own suffering in neatly compiled volume after volume of letters, memoranda and reports written in our own elegant longhand, in the process creating the first complete bureaucratic record of a totalitarian state that was Van Diemen's Land.

We were the convict-stockmen and the convict-shepherds in remote huts who murdered Aboriginal people and were murdered by Aboriginal people who were also us. We took our own convict-children away and sent our own convict-mothers back to wet nurse the free settlers' children when not being raped by the free settlers. We were, we are, we will and no one is exempt from the guilt: for we as Aboriginal people were our own blacktracker hunting down Musquito who had in turn hunted down others. Were, are, will be Black Mary Cockerill who—under God knows what forms suffering took in 1818 when as a heavily pregnant black woman she was interrogated by white soldiers—betrayed her lover, Michael Howe, the last of the feared Van Diemonian banditti who fled the grazier he had been assigned to as a convict, declaring that "having served the King, he would be no man's slave," and we are Michael Howe, the bushranger, who shot Black Mary when the red jackets advanced on him using her as their guide, or so said the red jackets, and we are Michael Howe's severed head, black-bearded and bobbing in a gunny sack being carried back to Hobart Town to be shoved on a spike on Hunter Street for birds to peck at and the mob to spit on, and it is our spittle dribbling down into his eyeless sockets.

And thereafter it was we who bore the inescapable, ineradicable shame that was not ours and which would always be ours.

And of Michael Howe's fabled lost book of dreams and garden plans that he wrote in kangaroo blood and neatly bound with kangaroo gut? We are that too. He wrote, is writing, will write, waiting for us to become a new, better story.

11

My first Oxford supervisor, a celebrated left-wing historian, on learning I had published a book of Australian history, asked what history has Australia, what culture. He was smiling. It was a statement, not a question, the implication clear. Not a block away stood a long house full of one of the biggest collections of stolen heads in the world, the Pitt Rivers Museum, among which were Tasmanian heads.

"Women smell like slime, don't you think," a fellow student told me, also not a question. Women had only been admitted to my college a few years before I arrived. In an Indian restaurant on the Broad, they confidently called for service: "Hey, Paki—oi! You filthy black cunt, here!" "Go home to the colonies, convict," my second Oxford supervisor wrote at the bottom of one of my essays. "This is feminism gone lunatic."

I worried it was me, a failing I could not name, some absence, something fundamental I did not have and which those all around me who were so assured, did. Perhaps it was so, I thought. Perhaps I was less.

12

I searched for what might sustain me. That proved not to be London, which I found an alluring promise often made but rarely kept. I sought some wild country to escape the claustrophobia, some larger world.

There was nothing. The rivers were sewers no one found unusual, the sky a haze of fine smog no one any longer saw obscuring the mid and far distance. There was a long-ago poisoned land, domesticated and dead, full of the sounds of diesel and the odour of chemicals, that people nevertheless regarded as bucolic and Edenic. Agri-business, highways, signs, industrial noise, a weeping urban sore metastasising into something that brought on only the impulse to flee.

There was no light there, no largeness.

No one noticed anything because no one any longer knew all that was irretrievably lost. No one saw that the paintings of Turner used a different palette for the sun to depict its original light in its lemon yellows and delicate hues of pink and coral in a time before that too was lost, refracted through the growing pollution into apocalyptic reds. A general numbness prevailed. The world there was grey, the world seemed petrified by its own collapse, at once dreary and dispirited, rectangle after warehouse after polytube, its cultivated and domesticated symmetries endless.

13

At my Oxford college, where mediocrity was a virtue called tradition, there was a law don regarded as uncharacteristically brilliant. I had assumed from his implausible upper-class accent, all Germanic *ho-kay ya* and choppy rhythms, to his baggy cords and tweeds and old fogeyish deportment, that he too was a Martian. But they knew who he really was. They had always known. They called him what he was, his torment, his inescapable origin, for he was, as everyone said without rancour behind his back, as the matter of fact and truth it undoubtedly was to them: *the dirty little East End Jew.* He would have been better with no home and two bags always packed, ready to leave for the next country.

It was what was celebrated as a sense of humour, as wit, it always was and always would be and its name was Oxford, it was a destroyer of worlds and always was and it always would be. The more the law don modelled himself on them the greater the gulf grew between their status and his origins, and the more he cultivated them the more they despised him.

14

Meanwhile, the Bullers wandered the Oxford streets, dressed absurdly as themselves or offensively as Nazis and after dinner had the whores in. The Buller B— who would be prime minister wanted me to be his wingman when he ran a second time for Oxford Union president, one more whore. I told him I couldn't stand the Union, that I wasn't even a member, and why, in any case, would I bother? B— said when I ran he would help me if I helped him and so I repeated my original answer and B— fif-faf-fuddled because he really had no answer, no one did, he was charming and you couldn't believe a thing he said, it was good, it was the best, it was inescapable: I could play the Australian berserk, or I could pretend to be a Martian—but, of course, the Martians always knew who you really were. It was their method. It was their penal colony. I can see now that they were also, in their incomprehensible, terrifying certainty that was so pure it was almost a form of innocence, true Martians.

15

And so the moment always returned, the man trap was always waiting and the Harrow closing, blood runnels ready, and all I could do was write another sentence, another paragraph. Write and hope and write some more in order to squeeze out the hate that for too long consumed me. I would write a million words to forget, to escape, to be free. To learn I was no less than they. But for the longest time the humiliation remained.

I would say nothing for years and decades and wonder why I was silent, would, when asked about

Oxford, say something using the supposed language of Oxford, something subtle, witty, epigrammatic, *balanced,* and immediately regret it.

For that was not the language of Oxford.

Dirty little East End Jew. Go home to the colonies, convict. Women smell of slime, don't you think. Hey, Paki—oi! Fif-faf-fuddle!

That was the true language of Oxford, its necessary language of hate.

16

Many years after the story in which question 7 features, Chekhov wrote another called "A Case History." A doctor is summoned to visit the sick adult daughter of a factory owner. The factory is an oppressive, polluted place. The factory owner's daughter, who lives a life of privilege, is ill, which the doctor senses is the result of a no less awful oppression than that of the factory workers. He sees in her wealth the source of her unhappiness. He understands that the strong inevitably oppressing the weak is a natural law, an idea that the doctor knows exists in newspapers and textbooks. But he now wonders if it is a law at all, and not rather a logical absurdity, "when both the strong and the weak fall victim to their own relationships with one another and both are compelled to surrender to a mysterious power standing beyond human life, alien to man."

For a moment the doctor senses the tragedy in which all are enmeshed and from which none can escape. But he cannot find the words he needs to convey his insight to the factory owner's daughter.

In the hands of a lesser writer the story would end at this moment of epiphany. But not with Chekhov. For the doctor glimpses this truth only for it to then slip away from him. As he leaves, he hears the church bells pealing and the larks trilling, and he immediately forgets the factory and its wretched workers and the sick owner's daughter, and instead he thinks "how nice it was, on such a morning, in springtime, to ride in a good carriage with a troika and bask in the sunshine."

Chekhov's line that "both the strong and the weak fall victim to their own relationships with one another" has the ring of forbidden truth. Who would dare write such a line like that today? Who would dare even think it?

Chekhov's terrifying pity is also the truth of who we are. His doctor is the why behind Kafka's Harrow and, with it, the truth of the spectators as well as the victim, the factory owner's daughter as well as the factory workers, the tragedy of the Martians as well as all those they destroy. And when the story ends we are left with a further why behind that why—the unexpected forgetting that is both forgiveness and vengeance, failure and freedom.

When I imagine Chekhov, I see him in his final days, dying of tuberculosis, goatee-bearded and pince-nezzed, standing on a cliff top edge in Crimea. Then he topples and is falling and we with him, at once free and light, and for a moment aware of everything.

17

We cannot be what we cannot dream. And sometimes we discover that we live in the dreams and nightmares of others and we dream anew. I only write this book that you are now reading, no more than a love note to my parents and my island home, a world that has vanished, because over a century ago another writer wrote a book that decades later seized another mind with such force that it became a reality that reshaped the world. It was a story of horror that was his fear of love, complete love without measure or boundary, and he created in its place an idea of destruction without limit. In this way, the world begat a book that would in turn beget the world.

Without Rebecca West's kiss H. G. Wells would not have run off to Switzerland to write a book in which everything burns, and without H. G. Wells's book Leo Szilard would never have conceived of a nuclear chain reaction and without conceiving of a nuclear chain reaction he would never have grown terrified and without growing terrified Leo Szilard would never have persuaded Einstein to lobby Roosevelt and without Einstein lobbying Roosevelt there would have been no Manhattan Project and without the Manhattan Project there is no lever at 8:15 a.m. on 6 August 1945 for Thomas Ferebee to release 31,000 feet over Hiroshima, there is no bomb on Hiroshima and no bomb on Nagasaki and 100,000 people or 160,000 people or 200,000 people live and my father dies. Poetry may make nothing happen, but a novel destroyed Hiroshima and without Hiroshima there is no me and these words erase themselves and me with them.

Ten

1

At first I thought I would escape easily. I was twenty-one, in a kayak, guiding a party of rafters down the Franklin River. The river had come up overnight. After a few mishaps upriver with some of the rafters flipping their boats, I was intent on shepherding the party safely away from a threatening drop mid-river and towards the far right of a rapid where there was a clear, deep chute.

That's when I made my first mistake.

I let myself be caught in a sluggish current gathering above the drop. Warning others away from it, I drifted ever closer to the drop's lip. Not until I was almost at the fall did I try to escape the current and make for the clear chute on the right. It was too late. Confident in my ability to find a way through the ugly snarl of boulders the river smashed into below I spun the kayak around, straightening it to parallel with the river as I dropped over the fall's lip.

That was my second mistake.

The kayak's pointed nose slammed under a rock ledge at the fall's base and I was flung forward as the boat stalled mid-drop. Wedged in the rapid, a wild river rushing all round me, thinking the water would flush the boat free or, at worst, that I would be able to extricate the bow while staying in the boat, I now made my third mistake.

I stayed in the kayak instead of getting the hell out.

2

I tossed my body to and fro sideways to wiggle the kayak nose loose. But this only drove the kayak nose deeper into its stony socket. My rocking turned more desperate until my spray deck—the neoprene cockpit cover that seals the kayak interior from flooding—popped. The river flooded into the kayak, filling it in seconds with the force of tons of rushing water. I sensed the fibreglass behind my seat cracking as the kayak began sagging beneath me. It was folding in half. As the front half of the boat sank to the riverbed dragging me down with it, I felt myself disappearing beneath the rapid. Behind my back the broken stern splayed upwards towards the air, braced by the drop's ledge, jamming the kayak in the rapid. The kayak's rounded front deck flattened onto my legs from the river's force, trapping my knees behind the moulded thigh grips. The overwhelming power of the water against my back pushed my torso up off the kayak seat so that I wasn't sitting but hovering above it, fixed in place by my jammed, crushed legs.

The river was now rolling over me, a black plume above my head that transformed into a cascading flume of aerated white water beyond it, a small air pocket forming in front of my face, all that would keep me alive for several hours.

I quickly discovered that if I allowed the river-pour pushing at my back and head to press me too far forward, the river would slam me face-first onto the deck of my flattened kayak, my air pocket would vanish, and if I was unable to get back upright I would drown. But if I leant too far back the river would similarly slam me face-up into its flow and I would drown that way.

Bracing my torso against the torrent at my back, unable to lean backward or forward, unable to rest, I focused my being on balancing and riding the river's ceaseless power as best I could, keeping my body tensed at the angle best balancing its strength with the river's force while trying to avoid any energy-wasting movement, trying too not to think of the pain beginning to course through my trapped legs where the cockpit moulding cut into my thighs.

Maintaining such an artificial posture against such power quickly became exhausting. It required all my strength to defy the river with my body as if I was a boulder forcing the river to divert around me. But I wasn't a boulder. I was like one of those bowing, thrumming sticks you sometimes see stuck just below the surface of running water, vibrating violently until it abruptly breaks and vanishes into a small vortex.

I tried to weigh my rapidly worsening options.

Except I couldn't think of any.

Young and stupid as I was, I knew my strength was finite. The river was not.

3

I had to abandon the boat. I frantically tried to pull the kayak's collapsed deck up a fraction, so that I might free my knees and legs and thereby escape. It was impossible. I felt myself quickening—my thoughts, my breathing, my muscles, my senses as my mind and body tautened—ripe for some explosion of energy I could find no opportunity to detonate. It was no longer clear to me how I might escape. Only after every physical contortion was tried and then tried again and found to be hopeless did it dawn on me.

I was trapped.

My only hope now was other people but there was no hope there. I was the only guide. The rafters were friends but none had any white-water experience or would know how to mount some sort of rescue in the middle of a raging rapid. Only one, P—, an accomplished rock climber, had outdoor experience. But P— was not a river person.

I was alone.

No way out meant—and the knowledge was slow in forming because it was so extraordinary that for a time I could not frame it—it meant I could die. And the idea of dying was astonishing to me. It made no sense.

And yet it did.

I knew my entrapment was exactly how white-water kayakers of that era died—one had just the previous week on the Franklin, on a rapid a few days further downriver called the Pig Trough. When shooting steep drops the sharp pointed bows of the long fibreglass kayaks of the 1970s and '80s would wedge under submerged rocks, the kayak collapsing in on the kayaker, leaving their legs pinned into the flattened front by the tiny cockpits of the period. And the trapped kayaker, in the middle of a rapid or fall, beyond the reach of human help, would quickly or slowly drown.

4

After what felt the longest time, what felt an hour or more but was perhaps only minutes or perhaps was hours, a face miraculously shaped out of the river and burst into the air pocket next to me.

It was P—!

I was overjoyed. He was somehow dangling from a rope in the drop, suspended in the river's violent flow by the others who, he now told me, were on a small island upstream anchoring the rope. He had organised them and contrived this way to reach me.

I explained the need to free the boat. But after he found a precarious footing and tried, he couldn't shift it a centimetre. Nor could he free my body. What had seemed straightforward no longer was. How P— would now rescue me was not clear to either him or me. The force of water on us both, the difficulty of him getting a solid footing, everything conspired against a rescue. In those days there was nothing in the way of rescue tools or equipment or knowledge. There was nothing in our kit that P— could have used to saw me out of the fibreglass kayak. Nor, though he tried, could he break it.

He tried to free the kayak with me in it. With his considerable strength and a fierce determination he tried to prise the kayak loose of the boulder shelf in which it was wedged. He tried to drag the kayak back and out. He tried to drag me out of the kayak. Over and over, he would disappear underwater and try to lift the kayak from beneath in order that I somehow might be able to free my trapped legs, a feat, were it possible, that would have required superhuman strength. But he refused to stop trying. When one method failed yet again P— would return to another, sometimes with a calculated variation, sometimes in a desperate fury. I really don't remember the many ways and methods he tried. I only remember that none worked. He was a strong man, but the force of the river violently bearing down on us made his task impossible if not farcical.

I could not be freed.

Between these efforts he would sometimes leave the air pocket and somehow disappear upriver. I am not sure how he did that, whether he pulled himself up on a secured rope or had them pull him back up. But each time he returned it was clear to me that he was losing strength. Over the hours of his increasingly desperate efforts, the cold took its toll on even his determined courage. He was wearing only a thin long-john wetsuit, rendered irrelevant by the way the rapid would force open gaps around his neck and shoulders and cold water pour in, negating the neoprene's insulating effect and chilling his body.

So it went for several hours.

5

I say several, but I have no idea. I grew weaker. I began to struggle holding myself upright against the force of the river. At some point P— returned with some ropes which he tied around my chest and shoulders. In my memory these were cheap, thin cords, but perhaps P— had brought a climbing rope and used that as well, I no longer remember. In any case, in this way my torso was lashed in place, trussing me up like a chicken, with the rafters upriver holding the ropes firm to ensure I wouldn't flop forward to my death. There was nothing they could do to stop me flopping backwards.

P— disappeared again.

After an indeterminate time, he returned with another rope and another idea. The rafters upstream on the island would drag me out of the boat with the rope, pulling me back up the drop and out of the kayak.

The rope was tied around me. P— disappeared, the rope abruptly tensed and tightened as those far upstream tried to wrench my body out of the kayak with sheer brute force. But I was anchored by my trapped legs.

The effect was excruciating. When they began pulling hard the ropes ripped at my immovable shoulders and chest. As my body was violently stretched by several people my torso and head were pulled backwards and under the water plume. There I had to keep my mouth shut or the water would force its way in and drown me. I had to hold my breath and hope they would not go pulling so long that I ran out. But rather than pulling me free, my rescuers served only to jam my legs further by pulling my thighs and knees hard up against the kayak's collapsed cockpit coaming. My legs felt as if they were being torn apart in a merciless, one-sided tug-of-war. My frame could only extend but not move. Agonising pain shot through me, my arms, my shoulders, my hips and knees. When the ropes went slack, I had to fight desperately to pull my torso and head out of the river's pour and back upright into the air pocket.

There were more attempts. After each failed in turn, P— would again try securing my body with a different system of roping, seeking to flatten the angle of my body, to get better purchase, to ease my pain, to somehow render the impossible possible. I imagine now his knots, how beautiful they must have been, beautiful rock climber knots, brocaded and elegant and so definite. But I have no memory of them. I only remember the agony repeating itself, over and over. Even with P—'s beautiful knots my legs were too tightly trapped, nothing worked, the pain was worsening, and I grew colder and weaker.

6

I became aware that something was leaving me. It was a very concrete sensation, as real as this book. It was leaving me and it was also me that was leaving, rising, leaving the river, rising into the gorge, into the sky. It was exquisitely peaceful and calm there. There was no pain. There was no fear.

Looking down I noticed the rescuers far below, haplessly perched on a rock midriver, upstream of the fall in which a coloured helmet could be made out beneath the rushing river water. I knew, of course, that it was me. But it was also not me, because I was in the sky.

And with that, I was suddenly aware that I was leaving my body.

Below, they were now straining on the ropes that held me aloft, a still-living marionette, preventing me from flopping forward and drowning, but only for so long, only until with my strength spent my head lolled back and unable to pull it upright my mouth filled with the river and my throat filled and my lungs filled and I drowned. Something was leaving the me far below that was no longer me. Something was happening that had already happened and would forever after continue happening.

And then with a rush I abruptly fell back into the pain, the excruciating struggle to hold my head at the correct angle. I fought to hold it just so. I fought to hold me. So it began, the struggle between my body and me. But I was breaking, leaving, and each time I left it became that much harder to return.

7

I used the weight of existence to return. The crushing, punitive gravity of living, the impossible heaviness of reality, I used the all-consuming pain that I had somehow left to come back and hold me to the wet black rocks inside the roar of the rapid, the heightened, alive smell of heavily oxygenated air to try to stop that something that was not me and was me from rising and leaving. It had an inescapable lightness and my heaviness, the heaviness of the world and the heaviness of my pain, seemed ugly and stupid in comparison. It kept rising and rising and why should it and me with it not rise? The lightness of death seemed an irrefutable reproach to such weight.

8

I tried not to think of my mother and father. I felt shame, unspeakable shame, as if the fact of my dying was a betrayal of them in some fundamental, inescapable way. I found myself summoning the image of J—'s face to fill the water in front of my eyes, even though J— and I were finished, even though there really hadn't been that much between us in the first place, it was J—'s sweet face that was now everywhere in the water pouring over me.

To see them, my parents, to call for my mother would have been the end, and so instead I called J—'s name, saw her face fill the sky, the world, and called J—'s name over and over so that I would not call for my mother and die. To call for my mother would have so seemed like the end it would have been the end, I was sure of it then and I am sure now, decades later, that I could not admit it was the end, that I could not call for my mother, that this river, these rocks, this gorge and the narrow cliffs bounding it were to be my grave.

And yet I knew I would, and soon.

9

A subsonic thudding from above shuddered the water and throbbed through me. I realised there must be a helicopter hovering just above the gorge. I knew without knowing that I was being filmed for the evening news. Or perhaps P— told me. The thuds came and went and later returned. I knew without seeing it the story they were creating. I had seen it too many times before. A suppertime snuff story.

I am not sure if that's when I began screaming or if that was not possible with the water. I think I did or must have. I was so frightened. I feared people would know it and think less of me. I wasn't the man I wanted them to think I was, nor even the man I pretended myself to be. I felt seen by the world and in the eyes of the world I was a frightened worm, nothing. Given no one could see or hear my humiliation except P—, it is strange that I would care. But I did. Perhaps we never stop caring.

10

As the river coursed over me panic began unravelling me. I had built myself up from a child into an absurd idea that went by my name but the river washed all that away. I was a hollow lie. What remained was just flesh. I wasn't human. I was a terrified animal, alone in its man trap awaiting death. It was not possible to me that I might die. I did not wish to die. I was twenty-one. At twenty-one you choose things. You control them. But I was not in control. Death was. Death was choosing me. I was tormented by the knowledge I was to die in this way, I was very conscious that I would never see the people I loved again and that they would never see me. The wrongness of this tormented me, as if I were responsible. I understood now, after all P—'s ever more desperate efforts, that any attempt to be freed was futile. I wasn't brave or stoic. I gave in to the pain which I had fought to keep at bay. The river washed away any dignity. Fear ate me. It was a fear such as I had never known, a fear that was both physical and spiritual, a desolation as large as the universe into which I was now vanishing.

The river was washing me away.

P— was close to spent. I could sense him weakening, his efforts lacking the brute animal power of his first attempts. He would have been in the early stages of hypothermia. His initial optimism that he could free me had thinned to a dour refusal to give up. Beyond, I sensed a chilling of the wet air and a darkening of the water. The light was leaving the gorge and it was passing into late afternoon. All I could think was that soon it would be night. I wanted it over.

11

I kept drifting up into the sky where I was safe and not in pain or fear, and each time it was that much harder to find a way back into my tormented body. I told P— to have them pull him upriver and then to swim back down and as he plunged over the drop to grab my torso and roll me forward with enough force to break both my legs. That way then, with my legs broken, he might be able to pull my trapped body free.

At first, he didn't understand what I meant. He thought I was incoherent. Perhaps it wouldn't have worked. I don't know if it was even possible physically. It was most likely a ludicrous idea. All I know is that was the only idea, the only hope I had left. There wasn't much time. We were near the end and snapping my trapped legs was our last hope.

Finally, he said he couldn't do that.

That's when I told him.

And only when I heard myself saying it did I know it was true.

I am going, I said.

They were my words. I hadn't understood what was happening until I heard myself saying them.

I was dying.

But P— didn't seem to accept what I was saying. It is a very strange feeling when you begin to die, when you find yourself existing between both worlds, suspended between life and death, and death is infinitely attractive, gentle, light, and you are aware of this thing within you leaving.

I am going, I said once more.

And it was true. The power of death was advancing within me and the power of life was rapidly ebbing. Whatever was me kept rising, lifting, and I could no longer fight both the weight of the river, this heaviness of reality and this growing lightness that was taking me to where I was not suffering. Somehow P— finally understood. And once more he disappeared from the air pocket. I realised he was gone, that he could not help, that much as he had tried it was beyond him.

12

I could still see J— and I tried to hold on to her after he disappeared, but then she too was gone and I was alone for the longest time, and beyond, I knew, lay a river, which opened out soon enough into a larger river and then a harbour and then a sea. I saw the river in its entirety and the sea in its infinity. I wanted to go forward into it and join with the sea. It seemed necessary, it seemed welcome. It seemed like hope even if it was despair. I wanted in one way or another to return to the river and flow into the sea. I knew I couldn't stay where I was. That was intolerable. One further second was beyond human endurance. I was breaking. I was disintegrating. Much longer and I would not be whole. I was ready to return to the sky and the sea.

13

I heard P— next to me say he would try now, he was not gone, he was still there, he hadn't left at all. But he was very weak. He had done everything that he could and more. Perhaps it is not possible to break legs so easily. Perhaps it is. To this day I have no idea. Something was leaving me now and I felt something starting to rise out of me like an untethered balloon. Try as I might, I couldn't catch the string, I knew I couldn't pull that strange thing back. Everything that could be done to save me had been done. I was dying and I knew I was dying. I wanted P— to give up and leave me. I did not want him with his dour determination, his ridiculous hope. I did not want any more pain. I wanted to beg him to leave me alone to die. But he had done so much for me. It felt wrong to tell P— he couldn't try, given I would be very soon gone.

14

P— reached under the trapped, folded fibreglass kayak. Once more he tried to shift it as he had tried in vain to for so long at the beginning. Only now, his strength was gone. The sheer volume of water pressing down, the angle of the kayak and the way it was jammed, the absence of a good foothold, all had made the task impossible from the moment the kayak collapsed in on my legs. I was too far gone to tell him it was pointless.

But he would not give up.

Ever so slightly the boat shifted. The kayak that had, hours before, been beyond his powers and perhaps anyone's to lift now, hours later, when he was exhausted, somehow moved. And then it slipped back. My legs remained trapped. I was not disappointed. My senses were dulled, slowed, and I had another destination and it no longer concerned me that it was impossible. It just was. The boat had moved, but not enough. And then P— tried again.

The boat rose a fraction for a second time. But this time P— managed to hold it there, to stop it slipping back, and then, somehow, he lifted it further. To this day I can only think this: there was something miraculous about it. At that very last moment he had found some superhuman strength. Each movement was small, but the boat kept rising. Perhaps he feared if he let the boat slip back he would not be able to repeat what was now happening. Again, he held, again he lifted, and with a power he didn't have P— kept on.

The boat felt as if it were suddenly floating free but I knew this was an illusion. It was only P— holding it there and we had at best a few moments before it became impossible for him to hold it any longer. The ropes around my shoulders once again tore into my flesh and as I cried out my head was dragged back into the river's pour-over and my mouth was filling with water and I was drowning and still P— kept lifting and lifting and the boat kept rising. My knees suddenly came loose and my legs with them and the ropes went slack. I still remember vividly as my body twisted and I popped out of the kayak like a cork from a champagne bottle. Hit by the full force of the rapid with nothing to now anchor me I was thrown violently forward.

15

I found myself falling through water, rolling and tumbling as I dropped over boulders with the fury of the rapid tossing my limp body hither and thither, smashing it into rocks, lifting it, dropping it, pulling it deep down into boils, far beneath into the darkness. When I surfaced in a run of waves in the middle of the river, groggy, buffeted, unbelieving, I heard voices yelling out.

16

But when I closed my eyes in relief, to my terror I was still trapped in the kayak in the rapid—and with it the water, the chill, the pain, the terror, the cacophony of the rapid in which I was entombed. When I opened them I was free, floating down the river. I was confused. I could only understand what I saw. I thought it was one final trick of my mind. I didn't dare close my eyes, terrified that I would return to what I feared was reality.

I thought I was dead and this was some final vision, a last, cruel trick of a disintegrating mind.

17

People were scrambling over rocks towards me, yelling to me. I felt only numbness. I was unable to swim or acknowledge them as they rushed to me. My gear was somehow all ripped off me. I was naked. My body washed out of the waves and caught in a large eddy swirled towards the shore.

I remember staring at a slow-moving paisley of white river spume around my body and my body one more spiral unravelling. I must have floundered or swum, but I don't think so. Someone was dragging me into shore. I discovered I could not stand. My legs didn't work. An arm didn't work. There seemed to be people everywhere, movement all around me, excited words, serious words being quickly exchanged, important decisions being made, and yet at the same time everything seemed still and serene, as if the world and everything in it had stopped. Arms picked me up, held me, but I was only vaguely aware of them, of my shame; I was suddenly very conscious of being naked, of my shrivelled, tiny cock and aware that there was nothing I could do about it, that the glistening bronze stones and boulders studding the river were still and the water was not and I was not sure I was alive or if this was a dream and I was already dead, a lie of the mind in which I was being carried up a steep incline, through dense rainforest and then I was atop a cliff and hovering next to it a helicopter into which I was half passed, half thrown over the abyss into arms that wished to hold me.

None of it meant anything. Every time I closed my eyes I was back in the rapid and I knew all this—my rescuers, the chopper, my nakedness—was just a hallucination, the most bitter of sweet dreams.

18

I never really talked to P— again. P— saved my life and I had nothing I could say to him. There was no enmity nor the slightest hint of a quarrel. We just stopped mixing. I saw him a few years ago on Bruny Island and told him I was sorry for that. He seemed to understand. Any form of gratitude for having your life saved feels inadequate and false. P— is not a man for false emotion. Perhaps that was wrong of me. Some things though are large, too large for any of us.

I saw J— one night in a crowded pub. I had been drinking and I tried to tell her how she had helped save my life. Perhaps I had been drinking too much or perhaps J— had. Perhaps it was impossible to explain. I told her but I could not explain any of it. I wanted to thank her. J— was kind and perhaps she understood or perhaps she didn't or perhaps no one can. Perhaps no one can ever understand that you are here but not here, that there is a moment that bisects your life—cleaves your life in half to be exact—when you are leaving and know if you do leave you will never return.

I had returned.

That was all.

It was a solitary, incommunicable knowledge. Finally, we smiled at each other and left, ending as we had begun so many years before, in mutual incomprehension.

19

Everything and everybody became to me as if seen from a vast distance, as if they were inscrutable inexplicable insects doing inscrutable inexplicable insect things unaware that the very next moment they might be swatted or squashed. I had stopped seeing people as people. For the longest time I was still far above the river. I liked people who didn't want to talk about it. Because there was nothing to talk about. There were no words. That's the thing about words: they are not the same thing as life. We just pretend. And I couldn't.

20

I went to see places I had thought I would never see again. I went to see people I thought I would never see again. It was such a comfort to be allowed to sit in their homes, I sat in their small kitchens, their tired lounges, their blighted backyards and said little or nothing, warmed by the immense human goodness of others. I was astonished by the small everyday acts of kindness too easily dismissed as everyday.

I was astonished and soothed, and for the first time I heard their stories of love that existed beyond their asides and anecdotes and opinions, that resided in their food and drink and worn chairs and scratched tables and in their touches, their stolen looks, their averted eyes. It's a comfort it's a blessing, as my mother would say. No comma. The indescribable warmth of laughter the incandescent human comfort of being alive with others. The blessing of everything that lives everything that lives is holy.

No comma no commas ever a world without punctuation fences gates trespassing signs for a time that's where I lived there a borderless world there with stunned gratitude there

After a time these feelings faded.

I fell from the sky.

Commas returned, full stops. And with them fences, partitions, borders, the razor wire of relationships. But the memory stayed. The memory never left. Life thrills to life.

21

The doctors came and went. It felt more out of human curiosity than medical need, and fair enough. They were young and keen to know what it was like. I had no idea. I had been choppered to the mining town of Queenstown, not far from Rosebery where my mother first had read me stories of adventures on rivers in that little bungalow's bedroom around which rainforest now gathered. I had been alive and now I was dead dreaming I was alive, or I was alive dreaming I was dead dreaming I was alive.

Mmmm, I said, mmm.

I was an object of interest having survived, but having survived there was little demonstrably wrong with me. As far as the doctors could see, I was alive, not dead, and I would live. The wounds would be stitched, the problems with my legs and hands—the damaged nerves in my limbs, one leg and one hand as good as useless—these were transitory and would recover soon enough. My head was another matter, still stuck screaming in a distant wild river, but that was of no consequence. The nurses talked a little. There were questions about my leg injuries. There was curiosity about what it was like. I didn't know. I was still there. I do remember one doctor talking in an animated way about a corpse still in the hospital morgue, the kayaker who had drowned the week before on the Franklin. He wanted to see my leg wound, now stitched. The dead kayaker, he said as though staring at a spider in a bottle, had exactly the same leg injuries.

Mmmm, I said, mmm.

At one point I was him, cold and marmoreal white in the morgue. Every other time I closed my eyes though I was just me, back, screaming, trapped in the drop drowning. It was extraordinary: I shut my eyes and I was immediately in another world. The pain was real, the cold was real, the water all over me was real, the deafening noise of the rapid real, I was forever wet and chilled to the marrow, and the terror was absolute. The only thing that wasn't real was the hospital. The hospital was no more than the tormenting dream of a man who had died in a river.

The sensation of being trapped was not a nightmare but an inescapable, perpetual reality. My uncontrollable fear was in the nature of undeniable knowledge, as real to me as the door handle you turn, the chair in which you sit, the bed in which you lie. The only escape was to open my eyes and, once opened, not close them. I was dry and safe and warm and alive if I could only believe it. I could not. Therefore I was dying or dead, both of which were far more plausible and believable to me.

When exhaustion did finally take hold and I began to doze off, I would come to screaming and screaming until I was given drugs and fell back into darkness until the river returned. To some extent, I never lost that feeling. The flashbacks lessened. But they never stopped.

Against the doctors' advice I left the following day. The duty doctor wanted me to take a wheelchair but given I had to catch a bus that wasn't practical. My brother had sent some money to a local clothes store. Attired in cheap labourers' pants several sizes too big and a flannelette shirt, I staggered out on crutches as best I could manage, dragging my faulty leg and holding up my pants with my worthless right hand jammed in a pocket. As I hobbled along the main street to the bus pick-up, past rusting corro and rotten timber hoardings, the beat-up and decaying buildings of that dying mining town, I remember only the brilliance of the light.

22

I am trying to tell the story properly. For many decades after, I didn't. Or couldn't. I didn't tell it at all, which is its own untruth, or when, very rarely, I did, I would fumble the details which for so long I had tried to forget. It seemed to demand of me something I couldn't give or say or be. When I went to talk about it I was back there or rather there was here, and time had collapsed, and once more I was a screaming worm outside of myself. It was that way with me for many years.

I wrote my first novel not about what had happened. I wrote it to exorcise what had happened. In any case, I didn't know what had happened. I didn't know I had died. I didn't know it could keep happening. Only time would reveal that.

For decades after, I kept returning to the Franklin until I had run it seventy or eighty times, until I could no longer remember how many times, and every time I had nightmares for the preceding weeks, nightmares that didn't stop until we passed that rapid, and only then would I feel I had stared something down within me that had to be faced in order that I might live again. That I return should perplex me. But it doesn't, not after I have passed that rapid.

I am an old clock that once a year has to be reset to know what time is.

23

I met a woman in a bar one night who told me she had slept with the lead character of my first novel. She'd never met the author but she had heard he wasn't much of a bloke.

I said I'd heard similar things.

"An arsehole," she said.

"An arsehole," I said.

"Strange," she said, "how differently things turn out in a book, even when they are just the same."

"Strange," I said.

"That's what I am trying to tell you," she went on. "I knew him, the one the arsehole wrote his book about.

I slept with him. He wasn't worth a book. He wasn't worth a beer coaster. He was a joke. But it was him, no doubt about it. Except he never drowned."

Another woman rang me one day, angrily accusing me of having stolen her story for the book, demanding I tell her how I knew the exact details of how her best friend had died. How?

That's life.

After that, I knew that the truth wasn't the truth even when it was. After that, I understood that lying about your book is, at worst, more entertaining than telling the truth and is, at best, more truthful.

After that, I remembered the advice T—, the famous writer, gave me many years ago after my first novel was published: make a mask and wear it. "Wear the mask and you're safe," he said. "Wear the mask every day you are in public and never let them see your face."

24

My mother and father never asked me anything about what had happened. For that I was grateful. I had no words anyway. All I had was an inescapable silence that filled me and protected me. They were glad I was alive and that was that. No more, no less.

A few years later I won a scholarship that was seen to be prestigious and which would see me go to Oxford in Britain which was then still called Great. I went home to break the news to my parents. My mother was cooking in the kitchen and was pleased, if hardly overwhelmed. She suggested I tell my father who was out back in the garden because he would be interested. I found him doing what he mostly did as he grew older, turning compost with a fork, lost in thoughts and memories. I said I had some news. Without turning around he said that was good. What was it?

I told his already hunched back.

He kept on forking his compost.

"If you can meet with triumph and disaster," he said finally, reciting Kipling, "and treat those two imposters just the same."

I waited for something more, but there was nothing.

I was alive and I wanted to live. What more was there?

He forked the compost with short jabs that belied his age. I stayed waiting at his back.

I watched the grass clippings and the little sticks he spent hours cutting up with his secateurs being turned into the darker fecund peat, the worms writhing, the steam, his arms still working in a resolute if weakened way, the slow yielding of one thing to another.

And I started to laugh.

Epilogue

1

At night the beach rocks clattered, as the sea dragged the rounded cobbles out, drew breath, and then threw them back up the beach, so many clacking castanets. Each collapsing wave shuddered our shack with its slow sonic boom. As the sea lurched ever closer to where I lay in that vertical board hut behind the dune, a child of four in my cold bunk bed, on an old cotton ticking mattress with the two thin wool blankets our father allowed, it sounded like the end of the world.

Every night I feared that the ocean would finally smash through the dunes and flood everything. How would we escape when the waves broke our frail little home apart as if it were no more than a sandcastle? As I lay there terrified, the world was moving. I knew when it came time I must move with it somehow if we were to live.

The waves kept walking ever closer, drowning out any other sound and thought until sleep and wild dreams came and morning woke us and when we ran across the road, a rutted, bracken-lined track, and over the dunes, it was to discover, to my daily astonishment, that the ocean was once more far away, leaving a great expanse of silvered beach quietly glinting wonder in the early morning sun.

2

At one end of that long beach the Forth River entered the sea, its sometimes fatal mouth belying a gentle final strait. A few miles upriver, past the flats, was the town of Forth where, long ago, my mother's cousin Dan Healy was said to have ridden into an Orange Lodge meeting on a horse, wielding a whip, ending the meeting and closing the Lodge for good. We had no idea what an Orange Lodge was, but we knew cousin Dan Healy was equally famous for his power of curing warts just by staring at them. Beyond the town the river valley steepened and there lay a weir where people had drowned and in which their ghosts were said to dance by moonlight in the white water.

Some distance above that was a small shingle rapid, rushing water skipping over river cobbles, next to which I had sometimes camped and where, many years later, as a young man in the summer after I died, I returned as a ghost.

When night fell, I threw my groundsheet and sleeping bag beneath my old EH Holden wagon and lay down, head and shoulders poking out from beneath the battered rear bumper bar. A dew soon settled on everything, even my face, so wet it was as if it had rained. After a time, I rolled on my side and closed my eyes. I lay that way for a long time.

I thought of everything that had happened. In the depths of my soul there was simply *before* I died and *after* I died. I couldn't understand why *before* I would say one thing yet feel its opposite privately, nor did I understand why that opposite private feeling so often also felt untrue. *Before,* I understood nothing about myself, nor my relationship with the world. *After,* at this very moment, the world appeared before me with an extraordinary clarity, as real as the rusting exhaust pipe next to my face, as the stars beyond. I wanted to live in this clarity forever.

Yet I understood that this was impossible. Somehow the confusion, the falseness, the incomprehension not only of others but of myself, and all the pain these things brought, somehow this was also the very condition of living that would soon return. For now, it seemed enough—more than enough—to be for this one moment alive, to live this one moment that I knew would soon vanish but hoped might stay with me forever after, lodged deep in my heart, beside a river that moved for no reason and would not stop moving until it met the sea.

3

My eyes opened. I saw an infinity of stars above circling in a great parabola. As I watched I had the curious sensation that the Earth was rolling beneath me and me moving with it. The enormous velocity of the planet as it careered through space with the Earth's movement was as real to me as if I were riding a wild beast. I heard—and this shocked me—the planet breathing in and out as if it were some living thing to which I was clinging.

This sensation was so real I feared that now knowing it I might be spun off into nothingness if I did not hold on. I felt myself suddenly rolling off my groundsheet and onto the wet earth and throwing out my arms, digging my hands into the red basalt soil, clawing myself into it. I would not be thrown off the wildly moving Earth into oblivion. No matter how hard it tried to throw me off I was hanging on and I would never let go.

I lay there, clutching the earth like a mad thing, panting, hearing it breathe, astonished, hearing myself breathing in response. I wanted to go forward as part of that great movement, I wanted to live every day as if every day might end back entombed in water. I wanted to waste none of it. And as the world continued rolling through space with me hanging on, I could not believe my good fortune.

4

When after Oxford I returned to the Franklin River, that ancient rainforest, those spiralling tannin waters, I was happy, and then, and only then, did I feel I had come home. I had got a job as a river guide and my first trip was on the lower Franklin. We flew by seaplane into the Gordon River and walked the old gold prospecting track cut by Charles Gould in the 1850s over the Elliot Range to the Franklin. The day was humid, the colours intense, the sky a most complete navy blue, the browns and greens of the rainforest steaming in some strange equipoise of complete decay and riotous growth.

After some hours we crested a rise and we finally saw the Franklin far below, long, tranquil black stretches here and there ruffling white where the water raced over shingle banks. And I was so happy. I remember standing there, between those two rivers, and I see that I knew at that moment that I too was poised between my past death and my future life. M— was pregnant, I had run out of excuses about not writing, and it was time to begin. The rainforest steamed in the midday heat, we stood in the sun a few moments longer, looking at the faraway river, resting, perhaps we ate something or drank something, and I said little, too embarrassed or unable to express everything that swirled in my soul at that moment, and then gathering up what little we had brought with us, we began making our way to the water.

ACKNOWLEDGEMENTS

Some years ago I was sent a remarkable essay by a then-eighteen-year-old Yolnju woman, Siena Stubbs, about the use of a fourth tense in the Yolnju language. It was, in its own way, the equivalent of Szilard's traffic lights for my thinking, and it informs this book deeply. I am grateful to Siena, as I am to Greg Lehman for his insights into Aboriginal history and identity. My thanks also to Mary Voss, Majda Flanagan, Don Tonkin, Simon Bower, and to Catherine Hill for being a keen set of second editorial eyes. I am, as ever, indebted to my consummate editor and publisher, Nikki Christer.

Parts of this book have appeared in different forms over many years as articles, essays and speeches published variously in the *Good Weekend,* the *Sydney Morning Herald,* the *Guardian, The Monthly,* the *New Statesman* and my own *Out of a Wild Sea* (Sydney, 2013).

The known facts of H. G. Wells's and Rebecca West's relationship I have adhered to; their conversations and thoughts are though my own invention. I have sometimes used words of theirs, sometimes made them up and occasionally combined both. On their protean lives there is a library of material.

Primary among my sources were Victoria Glendinning's *Rebecca West* (London, 1987), Katie Roiphe's *Uncommon Arrangements: Seven Marriages in Literary London, 1910–1939* (New York, 2007) and H. G. Wells's *H. G. Wells in Love: Postscript to an Experiment in Autobiography* (London, 2008), the latter a fascinating memoir of Wells's sexual life at once transparent and opaque, unreliable and truthful, as revealing in its own way as is Rebecca West's magnum opus, *Black Lamb and Grey Falcon* (rep. Edinburgh, 2006). The remarkable writings that first made West's adopted name while still a teenager can be found in the pages of *The Freewoman,* a radical feminist journal of the late Edwardian era, and reward reading.

Unless otherwise stated, all references to Leo Szilard are taken from William Lanouette, *Genius in the Shadows: A Biography of Leo Szilard, the Man Behind the Bomb* (New York, 2013). It seems necessary to add that while his vision of a chain reaction at the Southampton Row lights is attested to by Szilard himself, his bath before it is pure fancy on my part. István Hargittai's *Martians of Science: Five Physicists Who Changed the Twentieth Century* was also useful (Oxford, 2006).

On the development of the atomic bomb and the Hiroshima bombing I have relied above all on Richard Rhodes's definitive *The Making of the Atomic Bomb* (New York, 1986). If definitive it is also disputed: on this subject no book can be otherwise. My account of Szilard's influence on Sakharov I also drew from Rhodes, this time his *Dark Sun: The Making of the Hydrogen Bomb* (New York, 1995). The fullest account of the *Enola Gay* crew's reactions to the bomb that I have found is the one given by Peter J. Kuznick, "Defending the Indefensible: A Meditation on the Life of Hiroshima Pilot Paul Tibbets, Jr." (*Asia Pacific Journal*, 1 January 2008, Vol. 6).

Of the end of the Pacific war, which some Japanese date starting from 1931 and Allied countries from 1941, there can be no agreement and only proliferating accounts. My principal references were Richard B. Frank's *Downfall: The End of the Imperial Japanese Empire* (New York, 1999), which posits one long-held argument, and Richard Overy's *Blood and Ruins: The Great Imperial War, 1931–1945* (London, 2021), which invents several new ones.

On the Tasmanian genocide, there is a fascinating historiography, but for an introduction Henry Reynolds's work, especially *Fate of a Free People* (Melbourne, 1995) remains invaluable. (Reynolds, it should be noted, disagrees with the use of the word *genocide* in the context of the Van Diemonian war of extermination.) James Boyce's *Van Diemen's Land* (Melbourne, 2010) reimagines the invasion then and with it Australia now. Tom Lawson's *The Last Man: A British Genocide in Tasmania* (London, 2014) makes clear British responsibility. Raphael Lemkin's own illuminating chapters on the Tasmanian genocide from his unfinished and unpublished history of genocide were edited by Ann Curthoys and finally published as "Tasmania" in A. Dirk Moses and Dan Stone (eds.), *Colonialism and Genocide* (London, 2007).

Collioure—Hobart—Moulting Bay, April 2022–July 2023

ENDNOTES

1 Yuki Kitazawa and Matthew Allen, "A Story That Won't Fade Away: Compulsory Mass Suicide in the Battle of Okinawa," *Asia-Pacific Journal* 5, no. 7, 12 July 2007; see also Haruko Taya Cook and Theodore F. Cook, *Japan at War: An Oral History* (New York, 1992), pp. 354–72.

2 Jeremy Bernstein, "The Farm Hall Transcripts: The German Scientists and the Bomb," *New York Review of Books*, 13 August 1992.

3 Anton Chekhov, "Questions Posed By a Mad Mathematician," *The Undiscovered Chekhov: Thirty-Eight New Stories* (trans. Peter Constantine) (New York, 1998), p. 180.

4 Pat Feeley, "Whiteboys and Ribbonmen," City of Limerick Public Library, undated, limerickcity.ie/media/whiteboys%20and%20 ribbonmen.pdf.

5 Rebecca West, "English Literature, 1880-1905," *The Freewoman: A Weekly Humanist Review* 2, no. 36, 25 July 1912, p. 187.

6 Frederick Soddy, *The Interpretation of Radium* (London, 1909), p. 239.

7 Shaun Usher (ed.), *Letters of Note: Correspondence Deserving of a Wider Audience* (Edinburgh, 2021), pp. 277–78.

8 Stephen Bourque, "Rouen: La Semaine Rouge," *Journal of Military and Strategic Studies* 14, nos. 3–4, 2012, ciaotest.cc.columbia.edu/ journals/jomass/v14i3/f_0027476_22450.pdf.